Arabs and the Art of Storytelling

Middle East Literature in Translation
Michael Beard and Adnan Haydar, *Series Editors*

Select titles from Middle East Literature in Translation

All Faces but Mine: The Poetry of Samih Al-Qasim
Abdulwahid Lu'lu'a, trans.

The Desert: Or, The Life and Adventures of Jubair Wali al-Mammi
Albert Memmi; Judith Roumani, trans.

The Elusive Fox
Muhammad Zafzaf; Mbarek Sryfi and Roger Allen, trans.

Felâtun Bey and Râkım Efendi: An Ottoman Novel
Ahmet Midhat Efendi; Melih Levi and Monica M. Ringer, trans.

Gilgamesh's Snake and Other Poems
Ghareeb Iskander; John Glenday and Ghareeb Iskander, trans.

My Torturess
Bensalem Himmich; Roger Allen, trans.

The Perception of Meaning
Hisham Bustani; Thoraya El-Rayyes, trans.

32
Sahar Mandour; Nicole Fares, trans.

Arabs and the Art of Storytelling

A Strange Familiarity

Abdelfattah Kilito

Translated by
Mbarek Sryfi and Eric Sellin

With a Foreword by Roger Allen

S|U

Syracuse University Press

First Paperback Edition 2017

17 18 19 20 21 22 6 5 4 3 2 1

Originally published in French as *Les Arabes et l'art du récit: Une étrange familiarité* (Paris: Sindbad/Actes Sud, 2009).

∞ The paper used in this publication meets the minimum requirements of the American National Standard for Information Sciences—Permanence of Paper for Printed Library Materials, ANSI Z39.48-1992.

For a listing of books published and distributed by Syracuse University Press, visit www.SyracuseUniversityPress.syr.edu.

ISBN: 978-0-8156-3518-5 (paperback) 978-0-8156-3371-6 (hardcover)
978-0-8156-5286-1 (e-book)

Library of Congress has cataloged the hardcover edition as follows:

Kilito, Abdelfattah, 1945–
[Arabes et l'art du récit. English]
Arabs and the art of storytelling : a strange familiarity / Abdelfattah Kilito ; translated by Mbarek Sryfi and Eric Sellin ; with a foreword by Roger Allen. — First edition.
pages cm. — (Middle East literature in translation series)
Includes bibliographical references and index.
ISBN 978-0-8156-3371-6 (cloth : alk. paper) — ISBN 978-0-8156-5286-1 (ebook)
1. Arabic literature—History and criticism. 2. Narration (Rhetoric) I. Sryfi, Mbarek, translator. II. Sellin, Eric, 1933– translator. III. Title.
PJ7519.N25K5513 2014
892.7'0923—dc23 2014027337

Manufactured in the United States of America

Contents

Foreword

Thanks to the initiative of Syracuse University Press, anglophone readers interested in the Arabic literary tradition have now been able to familiarize themselves with the writings of Abdelfattah Kilito, one of the most original voices in Arabic literary criticism and particularly in what may be termed its "classical" or, if you prefer a more chronological and less value-laden term, its "premodern" tradition of belles-lettres (that French term being as close as one can probably get to the semantic fields covered by the Arabic term *adab* in its premodern context). This book is in fact the third collection of his essays to be published in English translation, the previous two being *The Author and His Doubles* (2001), which discusses the status of authorship within the Arabic cultural milieu, and *Thou Shalt Not Speak My Language* (2008), a similarly insightful collection of essays about language and its translatability.

In the current collection, Kilito is concerned with the analysis of narratives from the Arabic tradition, and in the process he casts his net far and wide. However, as is always the case with his writings, each essay provides evidence of not merely his own intimate familiarity with the source text, but also of the sheer breadth of his readings around the text in its indigenous surroundings and, more often than not, with respect to other analogous texts from both the Arabic and European traditions. In both cases, he invokes premodern and modern illustrative examples. Kilito's preferred method always involves questioning the texts, challenging long-accepted interpretations of them, and even confronting his own reactions to them (as in his thought-provoking essay in this collection on his lifetime of exposure to *A Thousand and One Nights*). The resulting analyses are never less than insightful, opening up fresh vistas through which to examine or reexamine the narrative tradition in Arabic and fascinating avenues of comparison with other examples of the genres that he selects from contiguous cultures. Thus, al-Harīrī, the renowned author of *maqāmāt*, "assemblies" (an intrinsically Arabic narrative genre that predates the European emergence of the picaresque), finds his verbal acrobatics juxtaposed with those of the French novelist Georges Perec (whose novel *La disparition* is written without using the letter *e*); the mind of the equally famous philosopher Ibn Rushd (known in the Western world as Averroës), is accessed through an analysis of Jorge Luis Borges's story "Averroës's Search."

The volume carries its own subtitle: *A Strange Familiarity,* utilizing an oxymoronic phrase that can be considered typically Kilitoesque in the richness of its potential. After an initial chapter in which the motivations for writing, especially narratives, are discussed, we encounter a series of analyses devoted to texts that are indeed mostly "familiar," at least within what might be called the "canon" of Arabic literature and its expression in the form of literary histories. Thus, in addition to the already mentioned al-Harīrī, Ibn Rushd, and *A Thousand and One Nights* (which merits two separate studies), we have the translation of *Kalila and Dimna* by Ibn al-Muqaffa' from the Persian tradition of narrative; Ibn

Tufayl's *Hayy ibn Yaqzān*; Ibn Hazm's investigation of love and its symptoms, *Tawq al-hamāmah* (*The Dove's Neck-Ring*); and the polymath al-Jāhiz's renowned compilation of anecdotes concerning that most curious group within Middle Eastern society and its notions of hospitality and generosity, misers (the *Kitāb al-bukhala'* [*Book of Misers*]). The texts themselves are thus clearly recognized as important landmarks in the history of Arabic narrative, albeit a history that has lagged far behind Arabic poetry as a stimulator for critical studies. But in the present volume at least, what may be "familiar" about these works is rendered "strange" by the defamiliarization process that Kilito adopts in his essays. Rather than making any dramatic revelations here about the insights to be found in the individual chapters, I leave it to the reader to delve into them, discover the questioning postures that they adopt, and consider the ramifications involved in reinserting the texts into the various phases in the development of Arabic prose and its narrative tradition. To provide just one example of the tack that Kilito follows, are there no circumstances, he wonders, under which the status of the miser within Arab-Islamic society, duly described in al-Jāhiz's *Kitāb al-bukhala'* by means of multiple (and in some cases sequential) anecdotes, might serve to illustrate the more positive character trait of "thrift"?

Here then is yet another compilation in English translation of Kilito's penetrating essays on Arabic literature and its genres. Although its primary readership may lie with those who are already familiar with the texts he has selected, the refreshingly open posture that he adopts in his critical analyses should also be attractive to a much broader readership that may one day—*in shā' Allāh*, God willing—become more aware of the riches of the Arabic literary heritage and its important role in the history of Western literary genres at various stages in its lengthy history.

Roger Allen
Professor of Arabic and Comparative Literature
University of Pennsylvania

Preface

For a very long time, the Arabs have complacently considered themselves to be a people of poets, indeed, *the* people of poets. Poetry was the record of their lofty deeds, their claim to glory, their secret garden, their *diwān* (divan), in the several meanings suggested by the term.

But since the first centuries of the Hijra, Arabic poetry has been judged untranslatable. All poetry is, to be sure, resistant to translation, but in the case of the Arabs the problem has presented itself in an atmosphere of rivalry, of declared or covert conflict with other cultures. Partisans of Greek philosophy and advocates of Persian wisdom (the latter being oriented mainly according to rules of governance and questions of etiquette) readily acknowledged the marvelous nature of Arabic poetry but observed that because it could not be translated, it was of some benefit only to those who understood Arabic. By contrast—they would add with a degree of perfidy and a trace of bad faith—the discourse that was philosophical and sapiential could be easily conveyed and thus be of profit to everyone. So we have on the one hand seclusion within oneself and particularism and on the other hand an opening up to others and universalism.

Since that time, the status of Arabic poetry has scarcely changed. Europeans have neglected it, judging the tale to be the Arabs' principal contribution. Is it by mere chance that

Cervantes attributed the authorship of *Don Quixote* to an Arab, Sidi Ahmed Benengeli? In his study on the origin of the novel, Pierre-Daniel Huet [1630–1721] pays considerable attention to the Arabs, stressing the fact that they are experts "in the art of agreeable lying" (1971, 57). Antoine Galland [1646–1715], for his part, mentions that *A Thousand and One Nights* "shows to what degree the Arabs have surpassed other nations in this kind of composition" and "that in this genre we have not, up till now, seen anything so beautiful in any language" (1965, 1:21). It is significant that Galland did not find it expedient to translate the poems scattered throughout the *Nights*, "poems which, it is true, have their own beauty in Arabic, but which the French can scarcely enjoy" (1:320). This is not without ironic consequences: the Arabs considered themselves the masters of the poem, and yet here we find them raised, without their even knowing it, to the rank of the best storytellers in the world!

They would realize this, against all expectations, only around the middle of the nineteenth century, when they would take note of the extraordinary success of the *Nights*, which had been translated from Galland's edition into all the European languages. Having adopted the novel, the short story, and drama—forms that had by and large not been known to them before then—they set about renewing their literature. To bolster and legitimize this movement, they were led, in the footsteps of the "Orientalists," to reconsider their literary tradition. In the latter analysis, everyone benefitted from this recuperation, reinterpretation, and revalorization of the corpus of ancient narratives. Arabic literature, resurrected thanks to the "experience of the foreign" [*l'épreuve de l'étranger*], has been inseparable from European literature ever since.

But the convergence is necessarily based on a certain selectivity: for the most part, one tends to set apart and laud those Arab tales that have some kind of rapport with this or that European work. [On the one hand,] when a text does not betray such a rapport, it is neglected and doomed to splendid isolation: that is what happened to al-Jāhiz's *Kitāb al-bukhala'* (*Book of Misers*) despite the fact that it is a crowning work of narrative art, simply because one could not link it to Molière's *L'Avare* or to Balzac's *Eugénie Grandet.* On the other hand, works that are judged to have had a more or less pronounced influence on European literature have enjoyed a favorable press and are praised to the skies. That was the fate of *Kalila and Dimna*, linked to the fables of La Fontaine; the *Maqāmāt* (Assemblies) by al-Hamadhānī and al-Harīrī, linked to the picaresque novel; al-Ma'arrī's *Risālat al-ghufrān* (Epistle of forgiveness), linked to *The Divine Comedy*; Ibn Tufayl's *Hayy ibn Yaqzān*, the predecessor of *Robinson Crusoe*; and Ibn Hazm's *Tawq al-hamama* (*The Dove's Neck-Ring*), a precursor to *De l'amour.*

And it is only appropriate that these works constitute the principal object of my comments in the following pages.

A.K.

Translators' Note

In translating this book, we have tried to duplicate Abdelfattah Kilito's characteristic urbane yet pleasingly accessible style and to avoid the arcane and tortured idiom one often finds in hallowed studies and translations of early Arabic literature. To minimize intrusions and to avoid rhetorical clashes, we have, unless otherwise stated, made our own translations of brief phrases and passages quoted by Kilito from several French translations of *A Thousand and One Nights* (Antoine Galland, Jamal Eddine Bencheikh, and André Miquel), the Qur'ān, and other texts.

In rendering Arabic script into English, we have adopted the transliteration protocol of the *International Journal of Middle East Studies.*

Finally, we are indebted to the following people who read our translation and made very helpful suggestions: Abdelfattah Kilito; Professor Roger Allen, who also consented to write the foreword for the book; and the anonymous readers who evaluated our translation for Syracuse University Press.

M.S./E.S.

Arabs and the Art of Storytelling

1 The Prophetic Pattern

RECITE! In the name of your Lord, Who has created (all that exists)" (Qur'ān, 96:1) is the first pronouncement revealed to the Prophet Muhammad and, in a sense, the first commandment. God spoke to the Prophet in perfectly clear Arabic—not directly, but through the angel Gabriel as an intermediary. Understood this way, revelation may be distinguished from poetic inspiration. The Qur'ān clearly affirms that Muhammad is not a poet: "And we have not taught him [Muhammad] in poetry, Nor is it meet for him" (Qur'ān, 36:69). In Arabic, the poet is called *shā'ir*, which means he knows things that common mortals do not. Where does he get his knowledge? He gets it from an inspiring demon who is his personally and who whispers verses to him. The incompatibility between prophecy and poetry lies in the source of inspiration, divine in the first instance, demonic in the second (see Izutsu 1964, chap. 7).

Numerous pre-Islamic poems evoke the inspiring genie. However, after the establishment of the Arab Empire and the great cultural upheavals that accompanied it, this figure quits the scene and is thenceforth little more than a literary afterthought, a playful theme evoked on occasion—and not without humor—in prose texts such as Ibn Shuhayd's *Risālat at-tawābi' wa z-zawābi'* (The treatise of familiar spirits and demons). The poet is not considered the spokesperson of a demon and hence no longer considered the purveyor of supernatural knowledge. We remain concerned about the "mysteries of eloquence," but instead of attributing them to invisible beings, we treat them as purely linguistic phenomena and strive to elucidate them.

This evolution is due to the dissemination of writing, to the codification of lexicography, grammar, metrics, the tropes and stylistic devices of speech, as well as to the development of poetic criticism. The poet's knowledge shares common ground with the champions of these various disciplines. From that moment in time, emphasis will be placed on the mastery of poetic technique and compositional skill; the image of the poet inspired by an occult force is replaced by that of the poet following the recipe of an art (*sināʿa*). In this context, the metalanguage used to define the poet is significant: he is compared to a jeweler, to a goldsmith, to a weaver. Like any artisan, the poet gives a particular form to the matter at his disposal—language—and produces poems that are so many finely chiseled gems or richly embroidered fabrics. The world is a bit disenchanted by the disappearance of inspiring demons, but we try to rectify that loss with the splendors of rhetoric.

All things considered, the inspiring genie has not totally vanished. This invisible being that obliged the poet to be his spokesperson has simply taken on a new guise. Henceforth, he will have the characteristics of an authoritarian character whence all discourse, in verse or in prose, is derived.

This authoritarian element is easily discernible in *A Thousand and One Nights*. Going to King Shahrayār, Shahrazād knows full well that she can defer her death only by telling stories. But how will she implement her project? How will she kindle in the king a desire to listen to her? She "alerted her sister that, once she had arrived at the king's palace, she would send for her. 'When you arrive [. . .] you will then ask of me: My Sister, tell us a wonderful story that will cheer the evening. Then I will tell a story that will assure our salvation and free our country of the king's behavior!'"[1] The wish to hear a story is cleverly suggested: the king allows Shahrazād to tell her stories, with the result that he is unable to fall asleep.[2]

According to some versions, when Shahrazād interrupts her stories at the one thousand and first night, the king orders his scribes to write the stories down. Only he could make such a decision: one speaks or writes with the permission or by order of the king. It is worth noting that he entrusts the writing of the stories to scribes and not to Shahrazād, who, nevertheless, is cultured (she is in possession of a thousand "books").

To some degree, the process at work in the *Nights* is also evident in *Kalila and Dimna*. We learn that the latter's author, the philosopher Bidpai, had at first a strained relationship with the king of India, a situation that reminds us of that of Shahrazād and Shahrayār. However, as in the *Nights*, calm replaces the crisis, and the king, recognizing the loyalty and the value of the philosopher, orders him to write a book (specifically *Kalila and Dimna*).

We owe the Arabic version of this work to Ibn al-Muqaffaʿ, who in his preface suggests that the transfer of knowledge

1. Unless indicated otherwise, the source for the *Nights* is the 1991 translation *Mille et un contes de la nuit* by Jamal Eddine Bencheikh, André Miquel, and Claude Bremond. [*Translators' note*: The brackets around ellipses indicate that they have been added and are as given in Kilito's text.]

2. In addition to which, he never slept; the stories replaced sleep for him: during the day he tended to the affairs of his kingdom, at night he listened to Shahrazād. As for the two sisters, we don't know what they did during the day.

should not be aimed at everyone, at least not in the same way. According to him, *Kalila and Dimna* "contains a certain hermeticism whose meaning we should seek" (the ability to hold one's tongue, to keep a secret, is one of the important themes of the book). Hermeticism, dissimulation: this rhetorical ruse is not an isolated fact in Arab culture, far from it. We can mention, in this respect, al-Ma'arrī, who acknowledges several times that his great collection of poetry, the *Luzumiyyāt*, contains an esoteric message. We may also cite the mystics who direct their disciples not to reveal their visionary experiences. As far as philosophers are concerned, their writings are intended only for a few readers. In his *Decisive Treatise*, Averroës forbade the teaching of certain segments of knowledge to the masses (*jumhūr*). In Ibn Tufayl's "philosophical novel" *Hayy ibn Yaqzān* (The self-taught philosopher) we are struck by the recurrence of the words *secret* (*sirr*), *symbol* (*ramz*), and *allusion* (*ishāra*). We are here dealing with an art of writing dictated by prudence and the fear of persecution (see Strauss 1988). It is not always good to state the truth, nor indeed is it wise to tell it to the whole world; to reveal it is, in certain cases, a reprehensible act, susceptible of bringing about *fitna*, sedition, which can disturb the spirit of individuals and sow discord in the community.

In the prologue to *Kitāb al-bayān wa-al-tabyīn* (Book of clarity and clarification), al-Jāhiz, bent on protecting himself against "the temptation of the word," asks God to protect him on the one hand from fatuousness and insolence and on the other from oratorical inadequacy. To illustrate difficult elocution, he cites the example of Moses, who, as the Qur'ān attests, was at first loath to take the divine message to Pharaoh: "And my breast straitens, and my tongue expresses not well" (Qur'ān, 26:13). Unable, nonetheless, to avoid his mission, he implored God in these terms: "O my Lord! Open for me my chest, And ease my task for me, And make loose the knot (the defect) from my tongue, That they understand my speech" (Qur'ān, 20:25–28).

Writing is a risky enterprise, and one must take precautions to preserve oneself from the enemy lurking in ambush. What enemy? Every reader, writes al-Jāhiz in *Kitāb al-ḥayawān* (Book of animals), is an enemy. The writer should never forget that he is addressing a necessarily hostile reader and that their relationship is characterized by enmity. If the reader is an enemy, does it follow, then, that the writer is the enemy of the reader? In any event, the writer knows that he is the object of mistrust, which leads him to negotiate with the reader and to try to gain his good will. Al-Jāhiz is the Arab writer who is most concerned about this enemy with whom one must deal: he involves the reader in his enterprise and utters prayers in his behalf ("May God preserve you . . ."). At every moment, he turns to him to be certain that he has his attention and to arouse his interest. If we accept his idea, every writer is then in the same situation as Shahrazād.

One should be wary of others, but also, even more so, of oneself. We are our own enemies, and danger lies within us—in our own house, so to speak. A man endowed with understanding, writes al-Jāhiz, must know that his book is closer to him than his own child. A horrible notion: writing is more precious than a child! The temptation experienced by the writer is so strong that he is ready to sacrifice everything for his books. We recognize the famous Qur'ānic verse: "Your wealth and your children are only a trial" (Qur'ān, 64:15). No doubt, al-Jāhiz had this in mind when he noted that the writer is more charmed by his writings than by his children. He has replaced the riches mentioned in the Qur'ān with books (and we should point out in passing that the poets were wont to say that their odes were their daughters). The immediate result of this seduction is a delusion regarding what one writes. As a consequence, in one's own case one either fails to see the flaws in texts or minimizes them, just as one tends to close one's eyes to the unpleasant aspects of one's offspring. Now, what escapes the vigilance of the writer is precisely what will be most obvious to one's readers, who are, by definition, enemies.

No doubt one's distrust of oneself explains certain habits that at first glance are disconcerting—for example, the attribution of one's texts to someone else. Indeed, forgery is a most complex phenomenon in which political and religious explanations come into play. However, we cannot exclude the idea that it is also intended as a device to thwart vanity. By placing one's text under someone else's name, the writer is able to step back from himself and better resist the lure of discourse.

Taken to extremes, the "temptation of the word" results in a guilty desire to compete with the Book of God, which is unique in its genre and is perfect. *I'jāz* is "the technical term used to designate the inimitable and unique aspect of the Qur'ān" (Grunebaum 1971, 1018). In this regard, we should keep in mind that imitation is the foundation of Arabic poetry, particularly in the form of the *mu'ārada*, or imitation: we compose a poem using the same metrical scheme, the same rhyme patterns, and sometimes the same theme as are found in the poem of a predecessor. Originality often emerges in the addition of a minor detail, in a slight variation on a theme, in a mere trifle that surprises us. The *mu'ārada* serves an agonistic function: at first glance, it seems to pay homage to the predecessor, but in reality it is driven by a desire to surpass him. Behind the compliance to the model lies the intention to take his place. When the Word of God is in question, any such intention is blasphemous and condemnable; any text can be the subject of emulation except the Qur'ān, the only inimitable text. False prophets tried to emulate the Qur'ān; and writers who were free thinkers or who expressed heterodox views (Ibn al-Muqaffa', al-Mutanabbī, al-Ma'arrī, and others) were accused of having tried to vie with the Qur'ānic text. The vizier Sāhib ibn 'Abbād, whose epistles were cited as models of fine style and whose vanity, in addition, knew no limits, once involuntarily gave in to this temptation. In fact, he never tried to imitate the Qur'ān, but if we are to believe al-Tawhīdī, who hated him and drew a terrible portrait of him in *Akhlāq al-wazīrayn* (Satire of the two viziers), the idea had secretly worked on him. During a discussion with a great rabbi who contests the inimitable nature of the Qur'ān, Sāhib grows angry and becomes threatening. Dreading the worst, the rabbi then tells him, in order to soothe him, that he does not consider Sāhib's epistles stylistically inferior to the Qur'ān. Suddenly Sāhib calms down and, changing his tone, softly explains to his interlocutor that no one can compete with the Word of God. However, al-Tawhīdī adds, slyly, Sāhib's features betray a joy and a satisfaction that he is unable to conceal.

Another important phenomenon in classical writings is citation. Beyond its didactic function, it is often the pretext for a display of erudition; however, contrary to what one might first think, it is far from being an antidote to the indolence of writers who lack inspiration. According to Ibn 'Abd Rabbih, selecting texts is more difficult than composing them! The difficulty comes from the fact that the selected wording must be impressive in itself while being pertinently integrated in the context in which it is used. From citation to plagiarism sometimes involves only one small step, and—all things considered—plagiarism is an art, but rare are those who excel at it. The project of writing an inspired book, which would consist of no more than pure copy, is doomed to failure from the outset. Nevertheless, it was once successfully done: al-Ḥarīrī's *Maqāmāt* (Assemblies), whose components, according to the grammarian Ibn al-Khashshāb, are for the most part borrowings. Far from blaming him, Ibn al-Khashshāb sees in them signs of considerable merit! One of the greatest books in Arabic literature, if not *the* greatest, consists then of little more than plagiarism. The same grammarian adds that al-Ḥarīrī devoted all his life to the writing of his book, in other words accomplishing a perfect plagiarism. Decidedly, a plagiarized work turns out to be more difficult to accomplish than an original book. One might wonder if the desire of a number of writers was not actually to compose works that would be no more than a fabric made up of disguised citations, a skein of mysterious allusions that only connoisseurs could unravel. Meanwhile, being a means, dictated by prudence, to camouflage one's thoughts, citation does not provide shelter: it reveals in one way or another deep tendencies on the part of the one who uses it. In fact, the choice and the disposition of citations imply a meaning that reflects the responsibility of the *quoter*. It is in this manner that the temperament of al-Jāhiz is manifested in each instance in his writings because of the profusion of texts that he reports. The juxtapositions that he contrives sometimes border on the scandalous, as Ibn Qutaybah notes: "He [al-Jāhiz] said: 'the Prophet said . . . ' followed immediately by: 'Jammāz said . . . ' or 'Ismā'īl ibn Ghazwān said . . . ' such and such a shocking remark. The Prophet is too venerable for one to associate his name with those of these two [rather unsavory] individuals in the same book, not to mention on the same page, indeed one or two lines apart" (Ibn Qutaybah 1962, 66).

This brings us to the question of heresiography. The presentation of heterodox ideas is not perceived as an innocent gesture: it may lead to a result different from that anticipated by the heresiographer, by attracting attention to opinions that might have been forgotten had they not been refuted. Let us consider the heretical books that were condemned and destroyed and of which there still remain some fragments or traces in the very books that have severely criticized them. Citation arouses suspicions of complicity. How can one be sure that the heresiographer is not a two-faced hypocrite who, fearful of affirming certain opinions as his own, rather attributes them to some notorious heretics, all the while taking care to heap upon them the usual condemnations? According to his detractors, al-Ma'arrī would in this manner, without striking a single blow, spread some of the ideas closest to his heart. Yāqūt suspects al-Ma'arrī, for example, of enjoying the citation of blasphemous verses (without apparently realizing that he himself [Yāqūt] is, in turn, quoting the same verses!).

Now, as soon as this suspicion arises, every heresiographer risks arousing distrust and attracting reproach. In *Al-Munqidh min al-dālal* (Deliverance from error), al-Ghazālī describes the difficulties he encountered when he published a book in which he opposed theses pronounced by heretics: he found himself being blamed for having bolstered their arguments. His friends told him: "You worked for them! Without you, without your detailed study and the logic of your commentary, they would never have been able to clarify their thoughts." As al-Ghazālī says, one of the difficulties facing the heresiographer is the need he experiences, before attacking a doctrine, "to begin by exposing it"; and it is not rare for this exposition to reveal a coherent and dangerously attractive system. To al-Ghazālī, who maintains that he is obliged to refute innovation, one might reply: "Of course, but you have begun by citing their doubts, before responding to them. How can you be certain that one of your readers has not absorbed these doubts, without taking your response into account, or has read your response without examining it thoroughly?" (al-Ghazālī 1959, 86–87).

Classical authors usually claim to be writing under orders, and rare are the prefaces in which there is not an allusion to a silent partner![3] Just like Shahrazād, they needed the authorization of the king or that of a great person. Sometimes the encouragement came from a friend.

This topos, which recurs regardless of genre or discipline, is no doubt dictated by humility and prudence, but perhaps also by the desire to avoid appearing nonchalant and to lend the writing a semblance of urgency. At times, it might adopt a familiar or parodical discourse. The preface of al-Jāhiz's *Kitāb al-bukhala'* (*Book of Misers* or *Avarice & the Avaricious*, which is riddled with expressions such as "You tell me that . . ." and "You ask me to explain to you . . .") is presented as a conversation with the reader and concludes: "If you had not asked us for this work, we would not have taken the trouble to write it, and we would not have been exposed, through those writings, to injustice and punishment. If we receive blame or if our book is imperfect, the fault redounds to you; if we are provided with an excuse, we alone shall benefit [from this indulgence]."

With al-Tawhīdī, the order turns into a dramatization tinged with humor. In a long dialogue that constitutes the essential thrust of the preface to *Al-imtā' wa al-mu'ānasa* (Book of enjoyment and good company) he relates that one of

3. Ernst Robert Curtius saw the frequency of this process in European literature, ancient as well as medieval: "The modesty formula is often connected with the statement that one dares write only because a friend or a patron or a superior has expressed such a request or wish or command" (1973, 85).

his protectors, the mathematician Abū-l-wafā, having learned that al-Tawhīdī has had a series of conversations with a vizier to whom he had introduced him, grows very angry because al-Tawhīdī has not informed him of the content of their discussions. After heaping reproach on al-Tawhīdī, Abū-l-wafā threatens to sever all ties with him and even to do everything in his power to diminish the vizier's esteem for al-Tawhīdī. However, he adds that he will forgive al-Tawhīdī the offence if he writes down everything that was said during these conversations. Confronted with this directive, al-Tawhīdī can only respond. Moreover, this conversation provides an opportunity for self-promotion. It is true that al-Tawhīdī shows humility and considers himself unworthy of the task that has been entrusted to him, but the simple fact of the demand that he accomplish it elevates him and enhances his value. His competence is recognized and confirmed by a superior who has specially chosen him; it is patently a question of investiture.

In the case of al-Harīrī, the commission is imbued with mystery. Discussing how he came to write his *Assemblies*, he mentions that during a meeting some scholars underscored the decadence of belles-lettres, or *adab*, "whose lamps have gone out." The better to underscore this atrophy of creative power, they mentioned by contrast al-Hamadhānī, who, a century earlier, had written his admirable "assemblies." The present mediocrity was compared to the excellence of the past (an old topos: in olden times everything was better). A break had occurred, and it was necessary to renew one's ties with the past. In the midst of these complaints, someone suggested to al-Harīrī that he write an "Assemblies" of his own, based on the model of Hamadhānī's work—in short, a *mu'ārada*. Citing the weakness of his abilities and dreading becoming the target of criticism, al-Harīrī began by refusing this proposition,[4] but, faced with the silent partner's insistence, he could only comply, in spite, he said, of "a waning disposition and failing intelligence." This was another old topos: an affected modesty, but one whose display will be quickly refuted by another passage from the preface in which, while outlining the matter and contents of his book, al-Harīrī points out their merit in a boastful tone.

Who suggested that he write? Obviously a great person, of whom there shall be no further mention later and who is described only in an allusive manner: someone "whose suggestion is an order and who, when we obey him, is the source of much benefit." The names of several viziers were brought up in an effort to identify the person. We cannot rule this out, but if the order really emanated from one of them, why is al-Harīrī—who had every interest in mentioning the person's name—being discreet? Why would he deprive himself of certain support and an increase in prestige? We are here very likely dealing with what amounts to an oratorical procedure: since a book must open with the mention of a commission, al-Harīrī complies with the rule.[5] In the same way, he respects the topos of affected modesty, for no one would be inclined to take him at his word were he to declare himself incompetent.

However, the twist he gives to the order remains enigmatic. Perhaps we might go further and—without undue audacity—propose another hypothesis. Al-Harīrī gives a role to the silent partner: it is someone who gives an order. But, as for him [al-Harīrī], what role does he assign himself? What

4. Such an attitude is to be compared to Bidpai's, who plainly and with no false modesty accepted to write *Kalila and Dimna*.

5. "Innumerable medieval authors assert that they write by command. Histories of literature accept this as a gospel truth. Yet it is usually a mere topos" (Curtius 1973, 86).

image does he give of himself and what model is he trying to imitate? Not feeling up to the task he has been asked to perform, he tries to comply, as we have seen. Doesn't he mirror the experience of Moses, who dreaded taking the divine message to Pharaoh, justifying his attitude by citing his lack of eloquence? But we do not reject a divine order; the one who tried to do so—namely, Jonah—would have to repent. In the end, al-Harīrī also accepted. By trying to bring the moribund belles-lettres to life, he presents himself as a savior, and, in the same way that a prophet tries to reactivate the message of his predecessors, he himself strives to revive the teaching of al-Hamadhānī.[6]

The reference to the prophetic pattern appears once more when we consider the narrative by the biographers concerning the reception of a work. In the beginning, al-Harīrī wrote only forty "assemblies" (this number is not without significance), and with the hope of seeing its value ratified he went from Basra, where he resided, to Baghdad. But that city's *lettrés* did not pay him any heed, calling him an imposter

6. In order to better clarify this question, let us examine the case of the two Jewish writers of the Middle Ages, Salomon ibn Gabirol and Judah al-Harīzī. Both strove to promote Hebrew, neglected during their time in favor of Arabic. Ibn Gabirol (d. 1058) wrote a didactic poem in Hebrew about Hebrew grammar, whereas his predecessors wrote their essays in Arabic. He decided to write in Hebrew, he said, following a dream where a celestial voice entrusted him with this mission. This did not stop him from writing his *Fountain of Life* in Arabic! For his part, Judah al-Harīzī [d. 1225], in the beginning of the thirteenth century, after having translated Harīrī, wrote his own assemblies in Hebrew (*Tahkemoni*). The decision to write in this language is owing, he suggests, to extraordinary circumstances that remind one of the experience described by Ibn Gabirol. About "the near prophetic framework" of the literary production of these two authors, see Pagis 1990, 140–50.

and spreading the rumor that he had found the manuscript of the *Assemblies* in a traveling bag that some looters had sold him in Basra. In light of these protestations, they challenged him to prove his veracity by writing a new "assembly." He went into seclusion for "forty days" but was unable to write; the Baghdadis' suspicions were confirmed. After this crossing of the desert, he returned to Basra, humiliated and offended. (Without trying to force the parallelism, we might say that to confront the general incredulity is, in the Qur'ān, a characteristic of the relationship prophets have with their peoples.) Later, al-Harīrī succeeded in writing ten "assemblies" and, returning once again to Baghdad,[7] he had the satisfaction of seeing his worth acknowledged. That was the beginning of a glory that would never fade. He was spared no praise, sometimes hyperbolic in nature. When al-Harīrī, writes Yāqūt in *Mu'jam al-udabā'* (Dictionary of writers), claimed that his *Assemblies* were inimitable (*i'jāz*), no one raised any objections.

A famous commentator on the Qur'ān, al-Zamakhsharī, likewise thinks that al-Harīrī's work is a prodigious phenomenon. He creates a dithyrambic eulogy about it in the following verses:

> I swear by God and his signs, by the place and time of pilgrimage,
> that al-Harīrī's *Assemblies* deserve to be written in letters of gold.
> A miracle confusing to everyone, even as they are guided by the light of his lamp.

7. Al-Harīrī's peregrinations between Basra and Baghdad deserve a more detailed examination in the context mentioned here.

Nor did this stop him from writing fifty assemblies of his own. But, certainly out of modesty, he does not place himself on the same level as al-Harīrī and limits his ambition to sermons, sacrificing the pleasant genre (*hazl*) for the serious (*jidd*). In other words, he compares himself with al-Harīrī only in moral exhortation.

Why did al-Zamakhsharī launch this undertaking? No high official or friend asked him to do so. He indicates nonetheless that he is responding to the desire (*raghba*, *talab*) of a reader who likes this type of literature. But the real catalyst is of a different nature: al-Zamakhsharī had to deal with a supernatural silent partner; exceptional circumstances presided over the birth of his *Assemblies*. Everything started with a dream, he wrote: a mysterious nocturnal voice told him, "O Abū al-Qāsim! Written word and perfidious hope!" This brief message is addressed directly to him ("Abū al-Qāsim" is his nickname); he hears it at dawn, a moment when the day and the night are about to separate. It is not a vision, but a call, a summons. What is the origin of this voice heard during sleep? An angel? The author remains silent on this point, but the reader cannot help but think of the divine revelation transmitted to the Prophet Muhammad by the angel Gabriel. In any event, al-Zamakhsharī awoke prey to a great fear and began right away to work on an elaboration of the received message by writing the parenetic *Assemblies*. The voice—let us be clear about this—did not order him to write; it issued only a cautionary note by invoking the imminence of death and the vanity of this world. Now, even though he was not responsible for a mission properly speaking, he interpreted the message as an instigation to write. "Recite!"—the Qur'ānic message revealed to Muhammad—corresponds in the case of al-Zamakhsharī to the order "Write!"

He therefore wrote the *Assemblies*, but it did not take him long to abandon his work, thus avoiding his task, like Jonah. Perhaps in the meantime he had some doubts concerning the origin of the voice; perhaps he felt unworthy of the grace of a divine inspiration. However, subsequently there occurred an event that reminded him of his duty: he fell very ill. After this second warning, there could no longer be any doubt; his sickness was a new warning, a second sign: he had escaped death, he had been granted a reprieve, and writing was his last resort. Shahrazād survived by telling stories, al-Zamakhsharī by writing the *Assemblies.*

For al-Zamakhsharī, the decision to write sermons coincided with the desire to start a new life. He renounced the world and broke with his old habits, fully resolved not to associate with high dignitaries and never to address any panegyrics to them. He abandoned his past way of life and left mundane literature behind him, thus realizing a radical separation similar to an emigration, a *hijra*: the rupture in his life, he wrote, was a break with *jāhiliyya*, a word used to refer to the period of ignorance, before the Revelation. And it is really a question of revelation: the words he heard while sleeping are not from him; he is not their author. Even if the book is written by him, the nocturnal message (which appears in the preface and at the opening of the third assembly) emanates from someone else and has the status of a citation.

The presence of the prophetic model is equally manifest in the case of Ibn Manẓūr (d. 1311), the writer of the famous dictionary *Lisān al-ʿarab* (The Arab tongue). Invoking the diversity of languages and colors that characterize his time (which is nothing new), he points out that his contemporaries are fascinated by the foreign language (*al-lugha-al-aʿjamiyya*) and neglect Arabic. What foreign language is he referring to? Because Ibn Manẓūr was living in Mamluk Egypt, one might conclude that he is alluding to Turkish. However, we may more logically assume that he is referring to Persian, a language that since the invasion of the Mongols had ousted Arabic in non-Arabic-speaking regions.[8] In any event, Ibn Manzūr paints an apocalyptic picture of the state of the Arabic language of his time: people distance themselves from it and despise it to the point, he asserts, that agreeable pronunciation, the beautiful accentuation of words, is perceived as barbarism or mere cacophony. Nevertheless, he adds, Arabic is the language of the Qur'ān and the idiom of the people of paradise, and its mastery allows for what no other language can provide: the exact knowledge of laws and rules (*aḥkām*) of the Book of God and of the tradition of the Prophet.

In this upside-down world, a heavy menace weighs on Arabic and, consequently, on Islam. By writing his dictionary, Ibn Manzūr aims to set things right and to save the paradisiacal idiom from shipwreck. But he feels all alone because no one is interested in his undertaking: "I made [this book] as Noah had made the ark, jeered at by his people." The catastrophe being imminent, he works to regenerate an earlier state of the language from which his contemporaries have strayed, but, like every prophet, he encounters doubt and becomes the target of mockery. As we might put it, he has to swim against the current. The deluge has all but submerged everything, but the Arabic language has survived, finding refuge in the "ark" of Ibn Manzūr's dictionary.

8. In these regions, "Arabic remained in usage only in the context of religion. For the rest, Persian dominates and finds a golden age of its literature" (Miquel 1981, 84). Let us point out that during his travels in the countries situated beyond Mesopotamia, Ibn Battūta spoke both Turkish and Persian.

2 How Should We Read *Kalila and Dimna*?

When powerless, one resorts to a ruse. That is the lesson we derive from *Kalila and Dimna* and the general corpus of fables that we learned in school. The lion does not need to resort to the tortuous processes of the ruse; his power gives him a clear advantage. Nonetheless, when he is threatened by another member of the same species that he deems more powerful than he is or when, weakened by age, he is no longer able to provide for himself, he has no choice but to resort to ruses, his sole means of survival. But when that time comes, is he still a lion?

The ruse implies a dual discourse, and thus in *Kalila and Dimna* we inevitably encounter references to the serpent, the animal with a forked tongue. Animals that populate the book hardly ever stop struggling, weighing the pros and cons of things, and arguing. However, we are not surprised to discover that the least talkative animal is the lion, whose speech draws its power from its limited use (for speech, depending on the status and rank of the one who utters it, will possess relatively different values and influence). Faced with a difficult situation, the lion makes those around him do the talking: he thus appears as the master of the discourse, not because he uses it frequently, but because he brings it about, allowing it or even demanding it.

In *Kalila and Dimna*, the goal of discourse is to establish the aptness of a point of view or cause and to convince one of the solid basis for an action. Yet it is necessary that the interlocutor be inspired to listen. How can you make him listen? By telling him a story! Assertion alone is not enough; it can function with a maximum of efficiency only if it is accompanied and supported by an indirect discourse, a narrative.

But who tells the story? We may consider two situations. In the first, the adversaries are peers—for example, two jackals—who alternatively tell their stories: of the two, the likelier to win will be the one who offers us the most persuasive tale. In the second situation, the interlocutors are in a hierarchical relationship, such as a lion and a jackal. Which then feels the need to narrate? Obviously the one who feels he is inferior. The lion sometimes listens to stories, but at no time does he tell one. What need does he have to tell a story, to try to persuade anyone of anything, when with a mere blow of his paw he can annihilate his interlocutor? The story is the weapon of the deprived, as we also learn in *A Thousand and One Nights*, in which the caliph never tells a story unless he is a fallen caliph.

Accompanying the archetypal narratives that constitute the essential material of *Kalila and Dimna*, there is a preface that has been attributed to ‘Ali ibn Ashāh al-Fārisi, someone about whom we know nothing. It tells us why the Indian philosopher Bidpai wrote this book intended for the king of India, Debshelim. Curiously enough, this preface opens with the story of the occupation of India by Alexander the Great. Why invoke that war episode? Why tell of the single combat that pitted Alexander against King Poros of India, a fierce battle that the Macedonian hero wins only thanks to a ruse? However, all things considered, this passage, which at first appears to be a digression, underlines from the outset one of the elements of the book—namely, hostility or confrontation. This is manifest in the content of the fables as well as in the variables of the composition and the translation of the book.

Furthermore, the same preface indicates that Alexander left India under the tutelage of a man whom he trusted completely. But the Indians, unhappy to "see an outsider, who does not belong to their kin, rule," stripped him of his power and replaced him with "a descendent of their kings," specifically Debshelim. But, as we shall see, the question of being a native to the area, a part of the family and the genealogy, and thus by extension the question of the familiar and the foreign are not irrelevant to the fate of the book, which was never meant to leave India, its country of origin, but which came to be disseminated throughout the entire world.

In *Kalila and Dimna*, there is no end to the evocation of the perils inherent in words: "Keep quiet, because therein lies safety." Bidpai, who knows this better than anyone else, nevertheless speaks out: he dares to address King Debshelim and to ask him to desist in his unjust behavior toward his subjects. Bidpai's own behavior, which is dangerous, has not been condoned by his disciples, but he considers it his duty to undertake it anyway: "We are not allowed, we wise men, to let the king persist in his wicked ways and in this life of shame." What he dreads above all else is that people will say of him after his death or the death of the king: "Bidpai lived in the time of the tyrant Debshelim, and he did not [do anything to] persuade him to change his behavior." He therefore goes to the palace, and, after receiving permission from the king to express himself, he invokes his [Debshelim's] ancestors: having acted well toward their subjects, he avers, they succeeded in "acquiring considerable fame" and "gaining the gratitude of men." Subsequently, he severely chastises Debshelim: "You are acting as a tyrant, an oppressor, and you are full of arrogance and contempt for your subjects[. . .]. It would have been better for you—and this would have suited you better—to take the same path as your ancestors and to follow in the footsteps of your predecessors, taking as a model those fine actions that they have left you as memories; ending the acts whose shame and ignominy are associated with you and which weigh on you; looking justly on your subjects; and adopting with an eye to their happiness an upstanding kind of behavior whose memory will outlive you and whose glory will leave behind a noble image of you."

According to Bidpai, Debshelim proves himself to be unworthy of his ancestors by not minding his reputation, the image he projects of himself in his life and that will remain in the memories of men after his death. The key word here is *glory*. God is not mentioned, or the hereafter; nor are there any allusions to eventual retribution or to punishment after death. God does not judge the actions of men; it is to posterity that the king will have to answer for his actions. This is the absolute opposite of the classical admonition (*wa'z*) that has had widespread credence in Arab culture, one in which it is unstintingly maintained that on the Day of Judgment every man shall have to answer to God for his actions. Generally speaking, the admonishment of the prince follows a request by the latter [the prince himself]: the lecturer then criticizes the prince's behavior, and the scene usually ends with tears being shed by the prince.[1] In *Kalila and Dimna*, things evolve quite differently: shocked by Bidpai's speech, Debshelim throws him in prison and comes within a hair's breadth of ordering his execution. Persecution befalls his "disciples and anyone holding the same ideas as he." Bidpai's fault—or his

1. For more details, see the next chapter, "Speaking to the Prince."

courage, depending on how one looks at it—lies in his having expressed himself directly and sincerely. He takes the initiative to present himself before the king and to talk to him with a single tongue rather than using the forked tongue of the serpent.

However, Debshelim later calls him back, treats him "with kindness," and recognizes his worth: "Oh, Wise and virtuous man [. . .] you spoke the truth." What seems to have been a very risky bet finally turns out to be a winner. Bidpai has been right despite what his disciples thought, even if his actions do not immediately bear fruit and have almost cost him his life.

Thereafter, it now being the king's intention to resemble his ancestors, he orders the philosopher to write a book for him, which, associated with his name and commemorating his reign, will somehow assure his salvation after death: "I thought very deeply, I searched the libraries where kings who preceded me had collected their books of wisdom, and I noticed that all of them had put in their libraries books that mention their lives' accomplishments and inform us of their behavior and [that of] their subjects.[. . .] I am afraid [for my part] lest [the day when] the irreparable [evil] that afflicted those men will afflict me, no book be found in my library [. . .] that might perpetuate my memory and bring to mind my name. I want you then to write for me an eloquent book in which you display all your intelligence.[. . .] This book will solve most of the problems which the art of ruling causes kings and me; I desire further that a book survive me, one that will in future centuries speak of my memory."

Once again, we notice that the discourse, be it written or oral, is dependent on the king. In the *Nights*, as we recall, Shahrazād had to play tricks so that Shahrayār would express the desire to hear stories—that is, authorize her to speak. Debshelim orders the writing of *Kalila and Dimna*, and the structure of the book itself reflects the royal command. Not only is that work in its entirety a response to the order, but each of its chapters reminds us of it, too: it is the king who establishes the topic to be treated. In the beginning of the first chapter, we read: "Tell me the story of the two men whose friendship, shattered by a treacherous liar, turns into hostility and hatred." So *Kalila and Dimna* is presented as a series of conversations between the king and the philosopher.[2] In writing it, Bidpai undertakes once again to correct and improve the prince, but he starts by modifying his own attitude. It is not wise to tell the truth; or it should be stated only respecting certain preliminary conditions. Thus, he will not address the king directly, as he had previously done when he admonished him, but rather in an indirect manner, through the filter of narration, hiding his teaching behind the fable.

As soon as the book is finished, the philosopher reads it before the king and his court, after which he immediately recommends a ban on its dissemination: "My desire is that the king—just as his ancestors did with their own books—order that this book be deposited in a safe place, and that it be carefully guarded. For I fear lest it leave India and fall into the hands of the Persians should they [ever] learn of its existence. Let the king order, then, that the book under no circumstances leave the library." Paradoxically, the book

2. This formula will be taken up again later—in a realm different from that of the fable—by *Al-imtāʿ wa al-muʾānasa* (Book of enjoyment and good company), in which various questions about literature and philosophy are tackled. This time it is a vizier who, during a stretch of forty nights, proposes subjects that the author will deal with. As in the Shahrazād stories, the discussions take place at night.

destined to celebrate the glory of the king must, like those written for his ancestors, be concealed and kept out of the reach of readers. Only kings and a few courtiers who have access to the library can learn of its existence. By making this decision, Bidpai condemns himself not to be read; he has written a book that is not to be opened. Put away, kept a secret, *Kalila and Dimna* is an unattainable treasure, buried deep in a cave and guarded by a dragon; whoever approaches it will die. In reality, Bidpai forbade its translation and its transmission, considering it "our" exclusive property. Now, if one refuses to be "translated," he is at the same time refusing to translate, and a brutal break is established with those around us. In this regard, we may recall that the Indians were very unhappy with the king who was appointed by Alexander to rule them: he was not one of them, and for this reason they removed him.

Translation is often presented as an act of love, a sign of openness, of tolerance, and it is with tenderness and nostalgia that we evoke the epochs in which it flourished—Baghdad in the ninth and tenth centuries, Toledo in the twelfth, and so on. However, the reality is less idyllic, the translation taking place more often in a context of competition and rivalry. Many peoples do not accept that their sacred texts be translated, considering the transition to another language to be a form of aggression (Steiner 1998, 329). The sacred text runs the risk of emerging from the process stripped bare, reduced to a corpse, to a skeleton; thus, it must not leave its language or quit its home. But Bidpai was not afraid that his book would be badly translated or somehow betrayed; he was not worried about uncertainties and vagaries that ordinarily accompany the transfer of a text. What he dreaded was that the Persians would appropriate it, assimilate its content, and glean power and glory from it. There is, in the very principle of translation, a polemical tendency (from [the] Greek [word] *polemos*, "war") and even an imperialist design, "a translation being a conquest" according to Nietzsche (quoted in Steiner 1998, 340). To translate is to invade a foreign territory, expel the people who live there or subdue them, and expropriate their goods and treasures. When we cannot overcome their resistance, we settle for swift incursions or for sending in a spy disguised as a scholar to bring back a copy of their intellectual production, as was the case with *Kalila and Dimna*.

Despite all the measures taken to protect it, the taboo book was translated into Pahlavi. The story of its translation is told in a chapter attributed to Bozorjmehr, the vizier of the Persian king Anūshirwān. Having learned of the existence of *Kalila and Dimna*, Anūshirwān "did everything in his power to acquire it, to make it his own, and to have recourse to it in order that he might govern and behave according to the wise directives it contains." A doctor, Borzouyeh, was given the mission to go to India to obtain a copy of the book and of "all the books the kings [over there] might need." It was a dangerous mission, but ultimately successful thanks to the complicity of an Indian "whom he was able to entrust with the task of recopying for him, secretly, at night, copies belonging to the royal library." That man was aware of the stakes involved in what the Persian doctor was doing: "You come to rob us of our valuable treasure, of our sublime science, and to take it to your country for the sake of the great pleasure of your king." It is true that by facilitating Borzouyeh's plan he was committing an act of treason toward his own king, but since it was a matter of translation, we are hardly surprised.

Borzouyeh's undertaking is a reprise of that of Alexander, with one difference: this time, the intent is not to conquer a foreign country and subdue its people, but to seize its intellectual treasures. In translating *Kalila and Dimna*, Borzouyeh in his own way conquered India. When he returned to Persia with this "priceless" bounty, he was received with the full honors he deserved, and the so long sought-after book that he brought back with him was read publicly in front of "the scholars and nobles of the kingdom." The translation of the book was celebrated, the same way its writing had been. But, in contrast to Bidpai, Borzouyeh did not ask that access to the book be forbidden.

If we now look at the Arabic version by Ibn al-Muqaffa', it is necessary to state that it imposed itself with such force that no one was really worried about its Indian original and even less so about the Pahlavi translation.[3] One should take note that if the original version of *Kalila and Dimna* as well as its Pahlavi translation owed their existence to the king, the version by Ibn al-Muqaffa' makes no mention in its preface of the Abbasid caliph al-Mansūr, who was his protector, or of any other silent partner. This is a bit odd. Does it mean that he took sole responsibility for this translation?[4] In any

3. Concerning the versions of the book, see Brockelmann 1978. See also André Miquel's introduction to his translation of the work. According to F[riedrich von] Schlegel, not to preserve the originals is typical of the Arabs, who, he writes, "have highly polemical natures; they are the annihilators among the nations. Their fondness for destroying or throwing away the originals when the translations are finished characterizes the spirit of their philosophy" (1998, 49). See also Benabdelali 2006, 60ff.

4. Our surprise increases when we notice that in two other works, *Al-adab al-kabīr* (Great learning) and *Al-adab al-saghīr* (Small learning), Ibn al-Muqaffa' does not mention a silent partner either. On the other

case, his version was not read in public, as had been the case with Bidpai and Borzouyeh, since it was not the consequence of an order.

In some respects, the situation of Ibn al-Muqaffa‘ is comparable to that of Borzouyeh: both made a foreign culture known, one by translating books from Indian to Pahlavi, the other from Pahlavi to Arabic, and their activities were undertaken in an atmosphere of distrust and either overt or latent conflict. But if Borzouyeh stole India's treasures, Ibn al-Muqaffa‘ gave the same treasures as a gift to Arabic culture, with the added value of Persian contributions. An ambiguous process, a calculated generosity. What would he seek to accomplish by further enriching Arabic, the language of those who conquered Persia? Does he wish to show the preeminence of the Persians, of the Indians, or, more subtly, of a book? What he has to say about *Kalila and Dimna* is in fact quite enigmatic: "When we know the book, we will be sufficiently enriched to ignore all others." Here we have a book that makes other books useless or superfluous. Every book will be full of lacunae, patently incomplete, but all the books together will constitute a single one: *Kalila and Dimna*, promoted by Ibn al-Muqaffa‘ to the rank of a supreme book!

One also needs to know how to read and, above all, to understand how this work was written. Thus, by mentioning the Indian fabulists, Ibn al-Muqaffa‘ specifies their way of writing: "Two combined reasons incited these scholars to make animals talk: they found in this device both [a means] to

hand, his *Risālat al-sahāba* (Epistle on the companionage)—in which, in a tone resonant with deference, he proposes some reforms in the political and military arenas—is addressed to the caliph (mentioned throughout in the third person).

express themselves freely as well as a vast domain to exploit. As for the book [itself], it combines wisdom with pleasure, the former quality making it the choice of philosophers, the latter quality making it the choice of those of lighter mind." This book, even as it stands integrated on its own, in fact consists of two distinct books—one manifest, the other hidden—and it is consequently open to two readings, one by the common mind and the other by the thoughtful mind. According to Ibn al-Muqaffa‘, if the reading process falls "short of a precise grasp of the book[. . .], then it is useless and uninteresting to its reader." Paradoxically, the model narrative, the instrument of the dissemination of knowledge, is in the end exclusively reserved for philosophers.[5] Thus, Bidpai doubly barred access to his book: not only did he forbid its dissemination by stashing it away in the royal library, but he also wrote it in such a way that its real meaning would remain hidden from the majority and be accessible only to a few privileged readers.

To access its deeper meaning, one must, according to Ibn al-Muqaffa‘, observe certain rules—avoiding, for example, any haste while reading: "We must not [when reading this book] jump abruptly from one topic to another without having fully understood the first, without having patiently read and fathomed it." One must be wary of the illusion of

5. The impediment to understanding refers back to the art of writing in the context of persecution, to borrow Leo Strauss's terms. In a context where persecution actually exists or threatens to occur, the ruse, a cunning discourse, becomes an art, of which the fable is an example. The mastery of this art does not, however, always protect one from the arbitrary. Ibn al-Muqaffa‘, the author of several works in which he lays down the rules of conduct to follow when dealing with princes, was executed under obscure circumstances in 757.

an instant comprehension. After all, it would take an entire lifetime to unravel the mysteries of *Kalila and Dimna*, whose simplicity is only superficial. Only an in-depth study will allow one to discover its encrypted teachings. Thus, Ibn al-Muqaffaʿ makes it clear that a good reading of *Kalila and Dimna* is possible only if one has grasped its allegorical scope. However, will he who is able to do so still have any need for this book?

3 Speaking to the Prince

Ibn al-Muqaffa' advised courtiers not to base their relationships with a new prince on their trust in his past character. As he wrote in his *Al-Adab al-kabīr* (Great learning), "Character changes with power [*mulk*]. Counting on previous association can prove harmful" (Ibn al-Muqaffa' 1964). That's what Falstaff did not understand: an accomplice to the dissolute behavior of the prince of Wales, he was brutally rejected once the latter became King Henry V.

In his *Muhādarāt* (*al-Muhādarāt fi al-Adab wa al-Lugha*, Lectures in *adab* and language), Yusī devotes a page to Ibn Abī Mahalī, the amazing character who claimed to be the expected Mahdī and who, after several victories over the Sa'di sultan, Zaydān, entered Marrakesh in triumph.[1] The tone of Yusī's page is somewhat critical or at least reserved toward Ibn Abī Mahalī, but its conclusion introduces an unexpected note: "It is claimed that his religious brethren (*fuqarā'*) came to see him after he had seized Marrakesh, in order to pay their respects and congratulate him. When they found themselves standing before him, duly congratulating him for conquering the kingdom, one of them remained silent. Ibn Abī Mahalī asked him why and urged him to explain.

1. About Ibn Abī Mahalī (d. 1613), see Berque 1982 and al-Qaddūrī 1991.

"For the moment you are a sultan," the man replied. "I will only talk if you allow me the freedom to tell the truth."

"You have it," replied Ibn Abī Mahalī, "so speak."

"Well, in a ball game," the man went on, "some two hundred men or more run after the ball, snatching it from one another, risking blows, injuries, or death to get hold of it. All it involves is moans and terror. If we take a closer look, we find out that it is nothing but *shrawit*, that is a ball made out of old rags." When Ibn Abī Mahalī heard this parable, he understood it and burst into tears. "We wanted to put religion right," he said, "but we went astray" (Yusī 1982, 262–63).[2]

In this scenario, Ibn Abī Mahalī is the recipient of two different discourses: a laudatory one delivered by a group and the other a chiding one delivered by an individual. The latter himself does not make the decision to speak; perhaps he does not even wish to speak, but his fidgety silence affects the ambient volubility and joy. For that reason, he becomes suspect and comes across as a spoilsport. It really is a joyous occasion. In any case, why has he come, if not to pay his respects to Ibn Abī Mahalī? Silence disturbs the atmosphere and causes discomfort. We are aware of the anecdotes about teachers who notice among their listeners an unknown young man who persists in not uttering a single word: all hypotheses may then be entertained. By standing out from the group, the *faqīr* is identified and draws attention to himself, primarily that of Ibn Abī Mahalī, "who urges him to speak." It is a command that he can by no means ignore. However, what he has to say may endanger his security: he knows that "for the moment" he is

2. Quotations are from Jacques Berque's translation *Al-Yosi: Problèmes de la culture marocaine au XVIIème siècle* (1958), 87.

dealing not with one of his brethren, but with a sultan; and he does not feel that he has the right to speak to him freely. If, for him, Ibn Abī Mahalī is a sultan, he is, himself, as far as Ibn Abī Mahalī is concerned, a subject over whom the latter has the power of life and death. So he seeks the *amān* (promise) that will assure him immunity. He asks to be granted the right to tell the truth. This implies that other people have lied. The truth is unpleasant; to express it is dangerous.

Even though he is protected from the potential wrath of the prince, he still does not address him directly. Instead he resorts indirectly to a parable, a proverb (*mithāl*). He uses neither the first nor the second person; in other words, he does not directly involve either himself or Ibn Abī Mahalī but rather sticks to generalities, invoking the derisory stakes of power, any power obtained through violence. Let us assume, however, that this is indeed the meaning of his parable, which is not at all certain. He remains allusive, merely proposing the image of a couple of hundred people running after a ball, getting excited by the game and hurting themselves. It is foolish because they are running after a ball made of old rags, but they don't think about that, engrossed as they are in the excitement of the game. It doesn't even occur to them to *examine* the ball.

Yet there's something else to examine: the parable itself, of which we should consider not only the literal, superficial meaning, but also the deeper meaning, the moral lesson. In general, classical authors make explicit the examples and parables that they use. This is not the case here: the *faqīr* introduces a riddle then falls silent, resuming his prior silence, one that is pregnant with latent meaning. The ball is now, so to speak, in Ibn Abī Mahalī's court. He is invited to examine it and ponder the parable and his own situation—namely, the appearance of power.

Strangely enough, Yusī falls silent as well—perhaps because the meaning of the parable is expressed by the *faqīr* himself—but he does so not after its pronouncement (as is usually the case), but rather beforehand, right from the very first words: "You are *for the time being* a sultan." That is an ambiguous comment, one that includes on the one hand recognition of Ibn Abī Mahalī's authority and on the other a suggestion that this authority will come to an end. Although the *faqīr* affirms his submissiveness and dependency, he also hints at the ephemeral aspect of the situation. Ibn Abī Mahalī has not been a sultan in the past, but he is "for the time being," implying a temporary, fleeting state. One day he will no longer be a sultan.

Ibn Abī Mahalī grasps the message. Dissolving into tears, he utters a memorable phrase in which he summarizes his entire adventure: "We wanted to put religion right, but we went astray." The intention that was impelling him was praiseworthy: he wanted to strengthen and reinforce the religion (*aradnā an najbura al-din*), but he ended up corrupting and ruining it (*fa athlafnā-hu*).

What is the significance of his tears?[3] One can see in them the recognition of the soundness of the *faqīr*'s words, a form of repentance, but perhaps he is also weeping for

3. Tears, writes al-Jāhiz in the book *Avarice & the Avaricious*, "are proof of thoughtfulness and sensitivity[. . .]. It is in crying that the devout come closer to God and implore His mercy.[. . .] Sufyān Ibn Muhriz [. . .] shed so many tears that he lost his sight. Many are those who were hired for [the ease with which] they cry. Among them are Yahya and Haytham, both of whom were nicknamed 'the tearful'" [translation from al-Jāhiz 1999]. People have been interested in the history of tears for some time. On their significance in eighteenth- and nineteenth-century France, see Vincent-Buffault 1985, 1991.

a lost innocence, he may have suddenly seen the painful truth—taught as well, by Greek tragedy and Shakespearean drama—that having power inevitably leads to guilt. Without realizing it, he has taken the wrong path; no longer himself, he is totally helpless when confronted with this situation. That is the way things work, and there is nothing one can do about it.[4]

In any event, and although this is not explicitly pointed out, Ibn Abī Mahalī's tears are *praiseworthy*: they signify a heart that is not yet hardened, one that, if not open to reform, is at least susceptible to the truth. This is a positive thing, a quality that seems to be prized by the narrator, even if, once again, he does not comment on the scene, a scene that, let us not forget, takes place in front of a large audience. Tears of purification, cathartic tears. It is as if Ibn Abī Mahalī's abuses were cleansed by this public confession—as if, after losing his way, he has found himself again and become, "for the time being," a *faqīr*, on the same level as his humble interlocutor. He is still a "sultan." However, as another author, Ibn al-Muqaffa', notes, power modifies the personality of the

4. Muḥammad Ifrānī reproduces the scene reported by Yusī, prefacing it with a passage that shows the transformation that took place in Ibn Abī Mahalī after his victory: "When Ibn Abī Mahalī entered the caliphal palace in Marrakesh, he did whatever he wished there.[. . .] The intoxication of power (*nashwat al-mulk*) went to his head, and he forgot the fear of God and asceticism upon which he had based his action" (1998, 207). "He did whatever he wanted in the palace": this expression, evoking arbitrariness, overindulgence, and abuse, refers to a well-known hadith: "If you have no modesty, do whatever you wish." By giving in to his passions and ignoring the rules of moderation and balance, Ibn Abī Mahalī is no longer subject to reason, or *'aql* (a word that is etymologically connected to the ideas of "tethering, linkage" and, by correlation, restraint and wisdom).

person who exerts it, but the function of the admonition is to force such a person to rediscover his past personality, his original innocence.

Original innocence? Indeed. In his work entitled *Islīt al-khirrīt*, Ibn Abī Mahalī evokes his childhood and the role played by his father: "Sometimes, when he had noticed my escapades, my passion for hunting sparrows, for playing ball, and for attending weddings, he would tie me up me with a rope and beat me."[5] This disclosure and the story reported by Yusī have many traits in common. First, there is the ball: Ibn Abī Mahalī continues to play ball! His escapades as a child evolve in his adult age into a life of wandering and uncertainty; from childhood to adulthood he does not change. Second, there are the weddings: the nuptials constitute an assertion of the masculine power of one who, through his nocturnal feats, draws attention and arouses admiration (Combs-Schilling 1989, 192–94). Is it not an analogous ceremony that now takes place, with Ibn Abī Mahalī becoming "sultan" and the crowd rushing to the palace to congratulate him? The sparrows must also be taken into account: they symbolize people of low status (*'awāmm*) who have followed him (Yusī 1982, 262).[6] Finally, let us point out the similarity between the father and the *faqīr*, the latter appearing as substitute for the former. Both punish Ibn Abī Mahalī: one beats him after tying him up with a rope; the other criticizes

5. Cited in al-Qaddūriī 1991, 39.

6. As we know, the ancient authors did not have a harsh word to describe people of low status, and the reference to winged creatures was often used. Yusī points that the masses follow every crow that caws (*nā'iq*). Inconstancy, instability, lightness: so many common traits between the masses and the sparrows. Don't we say *hilm al-'asāfīr* (literally "sparrows' forbearance") to mean idiocy, the stupidity of a dazed spirit?

him in order to bring him back to his senses, to the *'aql* that, once again, is a bridle, a fetter. The tears now shed by Ibn Abī Mahalī are akin to those he had shed when his father punished him.

Let us turn to another story recounted by Yusī in his *Grande épître à Moulay Ismaïl* (Epistle to Mulay Ismā'īl). This time, it involves Hārūn al-Rashīd and Sufyān al-Thawrī:

"When Hārūn was enthroned as caliph and the people came to him, he opened the treasury and began to distribute shares of it in hopes of seeing Sufyān arrive—someone with whom he had shared an interest in science. Noticing that Sufyān had not come, Hārūn wrote him a letter, which he asked 'Abbad at-Tāliqānī to deliver. When 'Abbad approached Sufyān, he found him with his companions in the mosque. When Sufyān saw him, he stood up to pray. 'Abbad waited until he had finished and gave him the letter. Sufyān did not touch it, but instead asked one of his companions to read it. It contained this message: "We have waited for you to come to us; we maintain the friendship and the relationship we have had," and so on.

Sufyān then told his companion: "Write on the back of the letter."

"But, Master," [the disciples] told him, "you should write to him on a fresh piece of paper."

"On the back of his piece of paper," he said. "If he acquired it in a lawful way, then so be it, but if he acquired it in an illicit way, it shall not stay with us and shall not corrupt our religion."

He then dictated as follows: "To Hārūn the lost, who has been deprived of the sweet attributes of the Qur'ān." He continued in this manner and then went on to say: "You have opened the treasury that belongs to Muslims and have distributed it according to your own desires. Have you received permission from those who are fighting for the faith? Have you obtained permission from orphans and widows?" And so on and so forth. Finally, he told him: "As far as friendship is concerned, we have severed it; there is no longer any relationship or friendship between us. Do not write to us in the future. If you do so, we will not read the letter or reply." After witnessing this, 'Abbad went to the market, removed his clothes, put on cheap ones, asked someone else to take the beast of burden to the caliph, and converted to God, the Highest. When he took the letter back to al-Rashid, the latter understood the moment he saw him.

"He who was sent has succeeded," he exclaimed, "and he who sent him has failed."

'Abbad then handed al-Rashid the letter. When he had read it, he dissolved into tears to a degree that inspired pity.

"Sufyān has behaved rudely to you," the individuals assembled in his presence (*julasā'*) said. "You should have someone bring him to you."

"Be quiet," he replied. "In this case the misguided one is the person you have led astray!" (Yusī 1981, 1:192–93).

This story shows many points of similarity to the preceding story. Suffice it to point out the characteristics that distinguish the former from the latter. The communication between the prince and the scholar does not happen orally, but in writing, which introduces a certain distance, first spatial (the caliph is in his palace, the scholar in the mosque). However, what is remarkable is the tone of Sufyān's letter, which is extremely audacious. Sufyān does not use any parable or formula of deference or prudence. He pushes presumptuousness to the point of refusing to touch the caliph's letter and having a disciple write the reply on the back of the same letter—and all this in public view. Sufyān is among his disciples (who are shocked that he does not write his reply on a fresh piece of paper), and Hārūn is surrounded by his usual entourage. This latter group reacts immediately, but the caliph silences them by specifically identifying the qualifier that Sufyān has attributed to him: "Be quiet. In this case the misguided one is the person you have led astray!" That the caliph weeps while reading the letter of admonition is already a good thing, but that he should scold his inner circle is even more praiseworthy, for he shows thereby that he understands the lesson and that he in turn is spreading the good word around him.

Yusī concludes this story thus: "Sufyān's letter is kept by Hārūn. From time to time he takes it out in order to read it." Yusī does not specify whether Hārūn wept at every reading or not.

Perhaps we can now grasp the purpose of the admonition—of all admonitions (*wa'z*): to reduce the recipient to tears. One day 'Umar ibn 'Abd al-'Azīz—whom Yusī admires as much as he does the "Rightly Guided" (Rāshidūn) Caliphs—heard a reprimand and "began to weep, scream, and groan, to such an extent that he almost died" (Yusī 1981, 1:253). Tears are the result of a fright (*khawf*); besides, ancient texts indiscriminately use the terms *wa'z* and *khawf* to point out the same phenomenon. "Admonish me (*'iznī*)," the Caliph Mansūr once told 'Amr ibn 'Ubayd (Sharīshī 1952–53, 2:182). "Frighten us (*khawwifnā*)," 'Umar ibn al-Khattāb told Ka'b al-Ahbār one day (al-Ibshīlī 1981, 105). In these last examples, it is the prince himself who calls for the words that will alarm him and make him shed tears.

Admonition is meant to make the prince cry, the same way that tomfoolery is meant to prompt laughter. It sometimes happens that the same person fulfills both functions. Buhlūl, for example, made Hārūn al-Rashīd weep and laugh in turn (al-Nīsābūrī 1987, 140–42). Tears as well as laughter defuse tension: the prince is then willing to satisfy every request, grant favors, and make gifts (which are generally accepted by the author of the joke and refused by the author of the reprimand).[7]

To better grasp the meaning and impact of the admonition, let us hasten to compare it to panegyric and satire. Panegyric comforts and stimulates, whereas satire annoys, humiliates, and offends. A satire by the poet al-A'shā "made 'Alqama cry like a [vile] female slave, he being someone who was normally too tough to cry and noted for his self-control" (al-Qayrawani 1955, 19). However, unlike admonitions, satire also tries to provoke laughter, for it presupposes an audience (listeners or readers) who enjoy the belittlement of the satire's target victim. A kind of complicity is woven between the author of the satire and others—everybody, that is, save one. No pity is shown for the victim, who is marked for life by the venomous barb. When it is aimed at the prince, he is the only one to suffer its effects. His followers, on whom it has no impact, most often react in anger: they are angry at the author of the admonition, who has *discouraged* the prince. But the latter takes full responsibility for this state of affairs, for, by accepting humiliation before God, he becomes ennobled before men. He gains a distinct advantage from the discouragement that has suddenly befallen him: his humility becomes an object of narration, a narration that will be retold and will elicit widespread admiration.

One of the models of admonition can be found in the episode in which [the biblical prophet] Nathan criticizes

7. Let us point out in passing that Napoleon wept after having heard a sermon by Father de la Rue. See Lavisse 1978, 709.

David for condemning Uriah the Hittite to death so that he, David, can marry his [Uriah's] wife, Bathsheba. Here we can recall the parable of the poor man's lamb and the effect that its narration has on David: he collapses and for seven days fasts and sleeps only on the ground (2 Samuel 12:1–23). Let us point out that Yusī likes to cite the following prophetic hadith: "The scholars of my community are like the prophets of the Israelites" (1981, 1:243). Because this prophecy has been realized through Muhammad, scholars are thus the keepers of the Message, and their role with regard to the holders of power must be analogous to that of the Israelite prophets with regard to their kings.

Yusī's essential points of reference are the time of the Revelation of the Qur'ān and of the Rightly Guided Caliphs; it is to that period that he turns in order to seek solutions to the problems facing the community. The truth is to be found in the past, in a short period that had shone with a vivid brilliance before disappearing forever. Thereafter, nothing is to be expected of the future: Yusī does not believe at all in progress; to the contrary, in the course of history he sees only regression and decline. This is a theme that haunts Yusī's work: many a time has he complained of being at the end of an era (*ākhir al-zamān*)![8] Indeed, history sometimes has pleasant surprises in store for us: an ancient truth might shine again (as is the case with the reign of the Umayyad caliph, 'Umar ibn 'Abd al-'Azīz, as Yusī points out). However, that is a mere accident, and it is not long before the night once again engulfs us.[9]

8. About this topos of the *convicium saeculi*, see Berque 1958, 83–84.

9. This nostalgia for origins is not new. Who is the scholar who has not lived history as an exile? About this topic, see Laroui 1986, 34–36.

The "imperative to do good (*al-amr bi-l-ma'rūf*)" is a duty of the scholar, but, according to Yusī, its practice must abide by two conditions: the probability of a favorable reception, and the guarantee not to provoke disorder (*fitna*). In the *Muhādarāt*, he severely judges the Don Quixotes of Mahdism, who, with the best of intentions (which, as he observes, are sometimes hard to distinguish from Satan's urgings), bring about anarchy (Yusī 1982, 256–60).

Let us tarry for a moment on the first of these conditions—namely, the likelihood of a welcome reception. On what might this probability be based? In this case, how might one make the prince accept a discourse whose goal is to correct and admonish him?

Yusī is well aware of the unfortunate consequences that such words might lead to. An old theme of *adab* has it that words can entail risks, particularly when they are addressed to a prince. It is better to remain quiet, but the paradox is that in order to recommend silence one must resort to words! The variations given by Ibn al-Muqaffa' on this theme are

---

In the case of Yusī, nostalgia is particularly stressed because it is double, involving the time of the beginning as well as the space of the country of origin. Yusī is a nomad, a man of the desert (*anā rajulun badawī*, he proclaims in his *Grande épître*, *Rasā'il* (1981, 1:170). As it is, he hates the city, which for him means narrowness, multitude, sedition, miserliness, and hypocrisy. In it, all good manners are disrupted: diet (excessive consumption of meat), the relationship between couples (the man loses his power to the woman, who becomes hard to please), paternal authority (children are affected by the corrupt lifestyle of the city dwellers) (Yusī 1981, 1:166–67). Conversely, Yusī paints an idyllic picture of his stay in the countryside: peace, innocence, generosity, and transparency. He reminds us that etymologically [the term] *bādiya* means what is visible, clear, outwardly apparent (1981, 1:182). The revival of rural space involves going back in time and creating ties with origins.

well known, as is his double recommendation (which he himself did not follow): first, hold your tongue; second, whenever possible avoid the prince's company.[10] Yusī, who does not refer to Ibn al-Muqaffa' but rather cites other sources, adheres strictly to the second recommendation. His position with regard to the first condition is less simple. He is aware of the virtues of silence, of abstention; but, as he notes, the person who remains silent "may enjoy security, but is not useful; he may even do harm by letting the sultan or someone else think that his quiescence implies that what they are doing is right" (1981, 1:154). Given that silence is a form of approval, it is akin to the discourse of flattery.

In the *Grande épître*, Yusī criticizes scholars who flatter princes and practice dissimulation in dealing with them. However, in the *Muhādarāt*, he praises goodwill (*mudārāt*) and cites many examples of scholars who in order to protect a higher general interest have shown themselves obliging toward heretics and Christians (Yusī 1982, 398–401). He avers that he too is by disposition inclined to be cautious about taking action, and he strongly disavows *mulāhāt*, the process of blaming and severely correcting others (Yusī 1982, 375). It is not always useful or appropriate to reveal one's true thoughts. If the discourse is addressed to the prince, tact is all the more essential.

Yusī's relationship to Mulay Ismā'īl is basically epistolary. Writing, let us recall, establishes a certain distance, the

10. In *Kalila and Dimna*, see the story of the ambiguous relations between the sage Bidpai and the king of India. We would also refer to Xenophon's *Hieron* and the remarkable study done by Leo Strauss, *On Tyranny* (1975).

sender and addressee not being in the same place. To this spatial distance may be added the temporal lag that separates the issuing of the message from its receipt.

An area where this remote relationship occurs is that of the *fatwa*, or consultation on a legal point. Four of Yusī's epistles are responses to questions posed by Mulay Ismā'īl, among them one concerning the captives of Larache and another one concerning the 'Akākiza sect (the two other epistles pertain to the status of women slaves). One of the functions of the scholar is thus to clarify the law and guide the prince's actions.

Beyond the confines of such "consultation," the prince continues to be the source of speech. Yusī's *Grande épître* is a response to an epistle by Mulay Ismā'īl in which the latter reproaches him for having, among other things, avoided his company. On the whole, this epistle by Yusī can be considered a treatise on the relationship of princes with scholars, on political power and what we might call discursive power. These two powers are, to a certain degree, separate and often situated in two different spaces, but they are frequently called upon to approach each other, join together, and come into contact. This is, indeed, the case with Mulay Ismā'īl and Yusī: their relations are indeed tense and fraught with conflict, but the simple fact that they write to each other is a sign of their desire to identify common ground.

Furthermore, the sultan's letter revolves around speech. It contains an order, a command: "If you have something to say, say it and reply to us point by point" (Yusī 1981, 1:232). Like Ibn Abī Mahalī's *faqīr*, Yusī is called upon to speak—assuming, that is, that he has "something to say," something that is not evident to the sultan, who seems to doubt his interlocutor's ability to compose a speech, to justify his position. Yusī is in the wrong unless he is able to reply to the sultan "point by point." There is no easy way out: if a point remains unexplained, his credibility is gone. More importantly, as long as he does not express himself in detail, he will be deemed guilty.

Yusī does even better: he ingeniously comments on the calling into question of his ability to speak: "What thing will I lack should I desire to speak? The language is Arabic, and I rely on what is induced by reason (*ma'qūl*) and transmitted by tradition (*manqūl*)" (1981, 1:232). By invoking his knowledge of Arabic, he the Berber (Amazigh), who is accused of having nothing to say, hints at the nuances related to the verb *'araba*: "To speak clearly, to use a clear and positive argument." By placing the *ma'qūl* and the *manqūl* first, he sets the two conditions without which discussion is impossible.

Nevertheless, it is not of his own accord that he has taken to writing. He claims that several reasons have made him defer his response for several days, the first being the mixture of veneration and fear (*hayba*) that he feels toward the sultan, something that reminds one a bit of the fear felt by the *faqīr* before he addressed Ibn Abī Mahalī. Initially, then, there is the temptation to remain silent, and yet Yusī, like the *faqīr*, is pressured into speaking by the sultan. He does not ask for the *amān*, nor does he explicitly refer to the pact that vouchsafes his security, but it amounts to the same thing. He reminds the sultan of the theme of the disadvantages related to speech, and above all he specifies that his hesitation to write to him is motivated by the fear that the sultan might think that he is trying to criticize (*murāja'a*), contradict (*muhājja*), or pick a quarrel with him (*munāza'a*). He takes special care to emphasize that he is only writing against his will, that he is only obeying the "order" issued by the sultan (Yusī 1981, 1:132).

What will the status of his speech be? He presents it as analogous to that of scholars when they comment on and discuss the speeches of authorities who have preceded them, without suggesting that this constitutes a denigration of the latter. It is in this same spirit that he himself will comment on the epistle that the sultan had sent him. He will embark on a debate with the sultan's speech, not with the sultan himself, or, as he himself puts it, "The speech is addressed to the speech, not to its author" (Yusī 1981, 1:133). To make this distinction between speech and author more explicit, he insists that the debate actually be engaged with the secretaries who wrote the sultan's epistle. With this allusion to secretaries, he lets it be understood not only that he would not question the sultan, but also that he is not even questioning his speech. It is as though Mulay Ismāʿīl were by no means involved in the debate but rather is to be situated outside of the entire affair. His role, then, is to be that of a *spectator*, a judge who will weigh and evaluate the arguments contained in the speeches of the secretaries and that of Yusī (Yusī 1981, 1:132).

Nor is that all. Just as he situates the sultan behind the secretaries, Yusī himself is placed behind the Ancients, the authorities of the past. It is indeed he who talks, but he makes sure that his speech is but an echo of what illustrious predecessors have already said. Whence the most important part of the citations in his epistle: hadith, sayings of the Prophet's companions, edifying history, proverbs, poems, and exemplary stories. Let us not forget that the stories of Hārūn al-Rashīd and Sufyān al-Thawrī appear in the *Grande épître.* By using the arguments of authority, it is not his own case that he is pleading; it is that of the Ancients.

Until now, we have seen the scholar obliged to write, be it to express a *fatwa* that the prince has asked of him or to defend himself against accusations leveled against him. In both cases, he *responds* to the prince. The initiation of discourse having eluded him, he finds himself in a secondary position. In some ways, this is a comfortable position in that the justification for taking up the pen is already established and ready to be applied.

The situation is different when the scholar decides to write to the prince when the latter has asked for nothing from him, particularly when he takes the liberty of composing an epistle in which he harshly reproaches the prince and reminds him of the principles of justice. Twice, Yusī gets himself into this situation: he sent one epistle to Mulay Ismā'īl (known as the *Petite épître* to distinguish it from the aforementioned *Grande épître*) and another entitled "Encouraging Kings to Be Just." Unfortunately, these two epistles are not dated, which makes it difficult to situate them in relation to one another or both of them in relation to the *Grande épître*, written in 1685 (AH 1096).

In "Encouraging Kings to Be Just," Yusī describes the transition of the caliphal government to an autocratic system. It is only in the last lines that he mentions the sultan, who, he writes, "loves the truth, searches for it, and never turns away from it" (1981, 1:255). The style, measured and circumspect, is one of *mudārāt*, affability.

In the *Petite épître*, Yusī is speaking from start to finish to Mulay Ismā'īl. This epistle, often cited, surprises us by its daring tone, that of *mulāḥāt* (reproach). It is an admonition in the style of the one sent by Ibn 'Abbād to the Marinid ruler Abu Fāris. As we have seen, admonitions addressed to princes are a genre that has credence in Arab culture, but for one reason or another this epistle by Yusī impressed his contemporaries more than any other (Qādirī 1977–86, 25–26).

People who deal with it today do so with a mixture of admiration and amazement.[11]

Yusī was well aware of his dauntless posture. The epistle is not lacking in attempts to lessen the impact of his criticism by the use of carefully phrased remarks. In it, we can find the traditional means of persuasion: propitiatory formulas, praise of the recipient, invocations in his favor, declarations of submissiveness and fidelity, oaths, and so on. However, what grabs one's attention is the fact that Yusī presents his epistle as though it had been ordered by the sultan himself: "For a long time, I have noticed that our lord has been searching for exhortations (*mawā'iza*) and advice (*nush*), and that he wishes to see the doors of prosperity and success opened. Therefore, I tried to write our lord a letter that, if he cares to take note of it, will allow me to hope for him the benefits of this nether world and those of eternity, as well as his elevation to the most glorious levels. And though I may not be worthy of uttering exhortations, I hope that our lord will be worthy of receiving them and will refrain from reproaching us" (1981, 1:237).[12] In an insidious way, Yusī is implying that his admonition has been written in response to a deep desire on the part of the recipient. In other words, the initiative redounds to the sultan.

In answer to the question whether it is better for a prince to be loved or feared, Machiavelli responds "that one should be the one and the other; but, because it is very hard to

11. See Berque 1958, 91–93; al-Jirārī 1981, 94–98; and the issue devoted to our author [Yusī] by the magazine *al-Manāhil*, no. 15 (1979).

12. Quoted from the French translation by Eugène Fumey (1906–1907), 111.

combine the two, it is much safer to be feared than to be loved if one can have only one of the two (2003, 71–72). For his part, Yusī suggests that the wise prince should not base his politics on considerations that involve affection because "people serve kings out of fear or greed, and such fear makes affection superfluous" (1981, 1:218). Emphasizing an old dictum, he affirms, in words reminiscent of those of Machiavelli, that "for the sultan [. . .] it is better to be feared than to be loved [*al-faraqu minhu khayrun min hubbih*]" (1981, 1:218).

However, everything proceeds as though the prince can scarcely be satisfied solely with the fear that he inspires in his subjects and as though he tries to conquer their hearts as well. Yusī knows this better than anyone: in his epistles, he proclaims his respect mixed with fear (*hayba*) for the monarch and also the affection (*mahabba*) that he feels for him. Thus, one has to believe that, in the absence of a blend of love and fear, power cannot be *absolute.*

4 This Verdant Paradise

There is, among the ninety-nine miniatures created by al-Wasitī in the thirteenth century to illustrate al-Harīrī's fifty *maqāmāt* (assemblies), a very intriguing one that represents an island. It is all the more disconcerting because it obviously does not correspond to the thirty-ninth "assembly" that it is supposed to illustrate.

In this assembly, the two protagonists, Abu Zayd of Saruj, the eloquent beggar, and al-Harith ibn Hammām, his faithful companion, sail for Oman. A tempest forces them to seek refuge at an island, where they go ashore to find food.

Which island is it? Al-Harīrī does not name or describe it. It is an island, and that is it.[1] However, for even the minimally informed reader, it brings to mind other islands, those that appear in *A Thousand and One Nights* as well as the one where Hayy ibn Yaqzān lands in Ibn Tufayl's "philosophical novel." However, there is a feature that links the thirty-ninth assembly to this novel: a difficult or unwanted birth. Hayy ibn Yaqzān, the fruit of a secret relationship, should not have been born. We should remember that at his birth his

1. No comparison here with Jules Verne, who as soon as he names an island, real or fictitious, provides ample information concerning its latitude and longitude, its geology, its fauna, and its flora.

mother puts him into a chest, a frail craft, and entrusts him to the waves. We have here the well-known theme of the child exposed to the elements who is miraculously saved, another example being the story of Moses. Let us not forget that in al-Harīrī's assembly the two protagonists barely escaped drowning. They too are saved from the waves.

In many stories, there is a connection between birth and the liquid element. It is also significant that al-Harīrī talks about a problematic birth, a newborn who will ultimately be saved. The two heroes, moving about the island, see the steel portal of a palace and some sad-looking servants. Soon thereafter, they learn that the wife of the master of the island is close to the end of her pregnancy but unable to give birth to the long-awaited child. The child runs the risk of dying (unless we consider that it might not wish to be born); and the mother is also in danger. At this point, Abu Zayd, a deceitful man, intervenes: claiming to possess a formula that facilitates birth, he prepares an amulet and orders it tied around the thigh of the woman in labor. What has he written on that amulet? A poem in which he warns the child of the evils that will strike him if he comes into this world. Abu Zayd advises him to stay where he is. And yet the child does not listen to this sound piece of advice. Even though he has been advised not to leave the womb, he hastens to come into the world. However, he arrives—if, that is, we can rely on Abu Zayd's poem—into a world that is not inclined to welcome him, a place where he will not be in his element. In other words, he is undesirable, as was Hayy ibn Yaqzān and, in one sense, Moses. There is also, then, an incompatibility, a tension between the human being and the world: their encounter can only cause trouble and confusion. A very pessimistic vision: the world does not need man, and man can only suffer in a world where he arrives uninvited. Happiness is in the maternal womb, birth being compared to a painful fall.

It goes without saying that the father of the child is overjoyed. He pays Abu Zayd generously and keeps him with him, but al-Harith ibn Hammām decides to continue his voyage to Oman. So the two companions must separate, not unlike the mother and her child. Upon leaving Abu Zayd, al-Harith, unhappy to find himself alone, has this horrific thought: "I would have preferred for the embryo and mother to die."

What will happen to this story at the hands of the painter, al-Wasitī? It is illustrated by four of his plates, which seems to be a particular privilege accorded this text. Al-Harīrī wrote fifty *maqāmāt*, so the average is in principle two plates per assembly.

The first miniature shows the boat at the moment it is about to set sail.[2]

The second shows the island (I shall come back to this one later).

The third shows Abu Zayd and al-Harith in front of the governor's palace: to the left, three aggrieved servants, to the right al-Harith and Abu Zayd (the latter carries a basket, a reminder of their quest for food). But what strikes us above all in this miniature is the depiction of the portal and the tightly sealed windows, whereas al-Harīrī's text mentions only a steel portal. Al-Wasitī, the illustrator, has painted three windows that are not mentioned in the text of the *maqāmah* (assembly). Why this addition? By emphasizing and multiplying closure, al-Wasitī stresses imprisonment,

2. This and the next two plates mentioned are reproduced in Müller 1979.

thus complementing perfectly the difficult birth: the baby is unable to find an exit.

The fourth plate[3] is probably more complex: top and center, the island's governor; to the left, Abu Zayd writing the amulet; and to the right, al-Harith holding an astrolabe. At bottom center we see the imposing figure of the woman in labor, a giant compared to the other characters. In fact, her proportions are so imposing that some people have viewed her as a fertility symbol (Ettinghausen 1962, 123).

Let us now return to the plate that constitutes the subject of our remarks: the one that represents the island, the garden-island. Al-Wasitī has painted something that has not been described; by depicting a landscape and creating a garden, he enriches the "assembly" and endows it with additional meaning. Why did he do that? Why paint something that does not appear in the text? It has been pointed out that he certainly got carried away by an imagination inspired by sailors' yarns (Ettinghausen 1962, 123). But by closely examining what he has painted, we are likely to find a profound connection to al-Harīrī's *maqāmah.* First, let us pinpoint what the plate offers to the eye. In the foreground, there is a pond containing four fish—beyond that, three trees, four monkeys, and four birds, one of them a parrot. Two of the trees, loaded with fruits, suggest abundance and profusion, notions that are in harmony with the fertility of the woman in labor.

But most astonishing in this scene are the two hybrid creatures who are moving about on the ground, turning their backs to each other and looking in opposite directions. The first one, with a woman's head and a bird's body, is a harpy.

3. Reproduced in Ettinghausen 1962, 121.

The second, endowed with a man's head (bearing a crown) and a lion's body, is a kind of sphinx or chimera. In Arab culture, the harpy and chimera do not seem familiar, but hybrid creatures are not absent from *A Thousand and One Nights.* In the tale "Hāsib Karīm al-Dīn," a character, Būlūqiyah, lands on an island covered with a forest whose trees "bore strange fruits that looked like human heads suspended by their hair. Some of the heads were crying, others laughing. Other trees had for fruit green birds suspended by their feet" (Galland 1965, 2:336). We see here that the usual separation between fauna and flora, between human and nonhuman, is being violated. In this same tale, as in "Hasan al-Basri," birds, abandoning their feathers, appear as young girls who are as beautiful as the stars (Galland 1965, 2:378). In that case, it is the separation of man and bird that is not respected.

Even so, there are no fantastic beings in al-Harīrī's *maqāmāt.* So what was al-Wasitī trying to represent? In any event, his miniature offers us the sight of two very strange creatures. It is strange to be an angel ["Etrange, être ange"], as Lacan would say.

One fact is certain: angels looked askance at the arrival of humans into the world. Let us remember what they said to God at the time of Adam's creation: "Will You place therein those who will make mischief therein and shed blood,—while we glorify You with praises and thanks (Exalted be You above all that they associate with You as partners) and sanctify You." Nor should we forget God's reply: "I know that which you don't know." (Qur'ān, 2:30).

Once again, nothing of this is mentioned in al-Harīrī's text. The island depicted in this plate is unquestionably an original creation, a personal contribution by al-Wasitī. How can one not see an Eden in this garden? It is an Eden where, at least at first sight, there is no tempting serpent; however, the unidentifiable tree in the center of the picture, which unlike the other trees bears no fruit, has a serpent's shape. But what is particularly striking in this Eden is the absence of any trace of an Adamic presence. This is an Eden before the advent of sin, before the creation of man, one that is self-sustaining and can easily forego the presence of human beings. However, man is not completely absent; he appears in the background, at the edge of the island. Indeed, on the plate to the left we can see the bow of a ship and a sailor; the anchor is visible, too, but it has not yet been cast. In an expressive manner, man has his back turned to the island; he has not yet set foot in the garden, but he is getting ready to land and to establish himself there, exactly like the child who, in al-Harīrī's assembly, is ready to be born, to come into the world.

5 The Exemplary Intruder

Hayy ibn Yaqzān

Arabic literature is said to have produced narrative works of great value, works that appeared suddenly and without warning. However, despite the promise that they offered, they never had a recognized legacy and remained in splendid isolation.[1] Even so, can we not say that, on the whole, a masterpiece is usually orphaned and sterile?[2] In this respect, the most interesting example is *Hayy ibn Yaqzān* (The living son of the vigilant) by the Andalusian scholar Ibn Tufayl.

1. This is more or less what Charles Pellat believes: "Il y a pourtant chez les Arabes des écrivains de talent qui créent des genres originaux et dignes d'être cultivés, mais, après une période durant laquelle de pâles imitateurs suivent l'exemple donné par le maître, le genre décline et disparaît ou bien on le détourne de son but primitif, on le dénature et on le traîne comme un pesant boulet" (But even so, there are some talented Arab writers who create original genres that are worth cultivating. However, after a period during which some feeble imitators follow the model set by the master, the genre declines and disappears, or else it is diverted from its original purpose; it is distorted and has to be dragged along like a heavy ball and chain) (1952, 22).

2. This comment can be justified by reference to both al-Jāhiz's *Kitāb al-bukhala'* (*Book of Misers*) and Abu-l-Mutahhar al-Azdi's *Hikāyāt Abī-l-Qāsim* (The story of Abu al-Qasim).

At first sight, what impresses us about this narrative is the mysterious origin of the hero: one does not know with any certainty if he was born normally, like other people, for Ibn Tufayl proposes two versions of his birth. According to the first, he was born through spontaneous generation, from clay in fermentation, on one of the "islands of India situated below the equator[. . .], an island where men are born with neither father nor mother" (Gauthier 1936, 20). According to the second version,

> Opposite this island there was another one of great importance, vast, rich, and densely populated. Its king, a native of the island, was haughty and of jealous character. This [king] had a sister whom he prevented from getting married. He rejected all her suitors, considering none of them a suitable match. But he had a relative [*qarīb*[3]] called Yaqzān, who married her in secret, according to a custom permitted in their religion. She became pregnant and gave birth to a son. Fearing disclosure of her secret, she nursed the child, then put him into a sealed chest. After dark, she carried him to the seashore, accompanied by servants and trusted friends[. . .]. Then she entrusted the chest to the waves. A strong current took hold of it, and that very night carried it to the shore of the aforementioned island.

Ibn Tufayl mentions these two versions without specifying which one he favors. They certainly diverge with regard to Hayy's conception. But both specify that he was brought up by a gazelle that had lost its fawn. Thus, whether Hayy had parents or not, he did not grow up within a family of humans.

3. I would translate *qarīb* as "relative" rather than "neighbor," which in my view does not conform to the context.

Just like the hero's gestation period, the genesis of the work is also an enigma. *Hayy ibn Yaqzān* does not belong to a known genre and is presented as being unique and without family. In the prologue, Ibn Tufayl points out that he intends to tell "the story of Hayy ibn Yaqzān, of Asāl and of Salāmān, who received their names from the master Abu 'Ali [Ibn Sīnā]." His book therefore is related to what Avicenna [Ibn Sīnā] had written about these characters. However, the kinship evaporates as soon as one reads both texts: one notices that the similarity does not extend further than the names of the characters.[4] Just as one may say that this work of Ibn Tufayl is born from that of Avicenna and thus has a predecessor, an ancestor, one can also say that it has no father or mother. The relationship between Ibn Tufayl and Avicenna is analogous to that between Hayy ibn Yaqzān and the gazelle that raised him. Hayy believes himself to be the son of this creature, which is false. As for Ibn Tufayl, he claims that his book derives from that of Avicenna, which is inexact.

Thus challenged, the reader is tempted to tame this wild text by placing it alongside others supposedly of the same ilk. Insofar as it deals with philosophical questions in a narrative framework, it has been considered to be a novel of a certain type. In this respect, the title of Léon Gauthier's translation is eloquent: *Hayy ibn Yaqdhân: Roman philosophique d'Ibn Tufayl* (Hayy ibn Yaqdhân: A philosophical novel by Ibn Tufayl [Gauthier 1936]). The subtitle introduces a detail obviously intended for the French and, by extension, for the European reader; it is a matter of bringing the unknown home to

4. On the relationship between Ibn Tufayl and Avicenna's *Hayy ibn Yaqzān*, one finds useful indications in Léon Gauthier's *Ibn Thoufaïl, sa vie, ses œuvres* (1909, 67–85).

the known, of facilitating access to the text by linking it to a category of the novel. This device is hardly a surprise: certain works reach beyond the boundaries of their primary soil and create unions with others, foreign and remote in space and time. Such is the case with al-Ma'arrī's *Risālat al-ghufrān* (The epistle of forgiveness), which has been compared to *The Divine Comedy* and al-Hamadhānī's *al-Maqāmāt* (Assemblies), which [in turn] have been linked to the picaresque novel. It is as though these works contain supplementary meanings that surpass the text itself, meanings that are imperceptible in their direct context, but that manifest themselves in an alien framework—in this case, a European one. Let it be said in passing that inasmuch as the novel genre is rare in classical Arabic literature or at best occupies a secondary place, the prestige of *Hayy ibn Yaqzān* only increases when it is qualified as a philosophical novel.

Léon Gauthier has linked Ibn Tufayl's text to later ones, to offspring it did not sire but that show a vague affinity with it. By qualifying Ibn Tufayl sometimes as a philosopher and at other times as a novelist, he has on the whole freed the work from its solitude. Nevertheless, this step can be realized only by integrating it into the family of the philosophical novel, a genre unknown to the author and his contemporaries. Ibn Tufayl certainly considered *Hayy ibn Yaqzān* to be an epistle, or *risāla*, a term denoting various forms of writing, but one that most often refers to a text where a question is broached in a personal manner (Tekin 1995)—in short, an *essay*. But this detail will scarcely enhance our information concerning this book's genesis. We shall always be encountering a hero with no family, ancestors, or descendants, one who, until his encounter with Asāl, considers himself to be unique.

It is "for stimulation and encouragement to make some headway," writes Ibn Tufayl, that he has had recourse to the narrative form, which he considers a veil that at once hides and reveals his thoughts.[5] After announcing in his preface that he intends to tell the story of Hayy, Asāl, and Salāmān, Ibn Tufayl refers to two verses that describe the function of Qur'ānic stories or the effects that they are supposed to produce: "There was certainly in their stories a lesson for those of understanding" (Sūrat Yūsuf, 12:111); "Indeed in that is a reminder for whoever has a heart or who listens while he is present [in mind]" (Sūrat Qāf, 50:37). These two verses entail two types of reception: the first confines itself to the exterior meaning of the Qur'ānic story, while the second searches for the deeper meaning. Placed at the end of Ibn Tufayl's preface, these two citations point to the method to be followed in reading *Hayy ibn Yaqzān*. The author suggests that his story contains hidden instructions and requires attentive reading.

From the outset, he declares that the story is borrowed from a prior discourse: "Our virtuous predecessors (May God be pleased with them!) said that . . . ," implying that he is going to limit himself to reproducing what predecessors have said. It is a matter of anonymous transmitters. What is striking is that he mentions them after stressing that Avicenna has *named* Hayy, Asāl, and Salāmān. If the characters of the story have names, the virtuous predecessors do not. What, then, is the status of their discourse? Because they remain unidentified, one can as a rule place only limited trust in them. Doesn't what they transmit belong to the same category as stories that do not stand on a solid foundation—that

5. Talking about the story of Hayy, Ibn Tufayl uses, besides *qissa*, the terms *naba'* and *khabar*. On the signification of these words, see Mallet 1999.

is, on an authoritative name—and that circulate without anyone worrying about their origins, like *A Thousand and One Nights*, whose stories begin with "It reached me that . . ." or "It's been reported that . . ."?

It is very doubtful that Ibn Tufayl had such tales in mind, even if affinities exist between his tale and the story of Sindbād: loss of parents, solitude, the boat, the sailors, the raft or chest carried off by the current, the uninhabited and inhabited islands, the voyage, and the return to the point of departure. On the other hand, Ibn Tufayl would not deny a certain affinity with *Kalila and Dimna*, which was for the Ancients a major point of reference whenever they were discussing fiction.

There are several elements common to both *Kalila* and *Hayy*. First of all, it is interesting to note that Ibn Tufayl, when speaking about predecessors whose discourse he has reproduced, uses not only "They mentioned" and "They said," but also the expression *za'amū* ("They narrated that"). Now, *za'amū* constitutes specifically the protocol for the openings of fables found in *Kalila and Dimna*! The fabulists are not named, but the work is placed under the authority of the Hindu philosopher Bidpai. One might say the same with regard to *Hayy ibn Yaqzān*, whose author, as we have already seen, relies on anonymous transmitters. Moreover, Bidpai and Ibn Tufayl after him envision two types of reader: those who take the meaning of the tales at face value and those who can elicit their hidden meaning. Finally, let us remember that before Bidpai writes his book on the orders of Debshelim, the king of India, he takes an initiative that will be repeated in different form in *Hayy ibn Yaqzān*: he tries to reform Debshelim and put an end to his tyranny. Although his disciples have warned him of the risks of such a venture (as Asāl will do with Hayy), he will not let himself be deterred.[6] He goes to the king and admonishes him in no uncertain terms. It will be recalled that Debshelim, furious at the philosopher's temerity, throws him in prison.

Bidpai attributes his fables to predecessors whom he does not name, but on whom he implicitly bestows respect and esteem. For his part, Ibn Tufayl, even as he, too, neglects to name the transmitters whose accounts he relates, explicitly describes them as "virtuous," and—the ultimate homage—in mentioning them he makes use of a formula usually reserved for the companions of the Prophet: "May God be pleased with them (*radiya-l-lāhu 'anhum*)!" What they have reported can thus under no circumstances be considered false or devoid of value.

What is most odd is that after having announced in the beginning of the book that he is quoting the virtuous predecessors (and after having, in the prologue, stressed his indebtedness to al-Fārābī, Avicenna, al-Ghazālī, and Ibn Bājjāh), Ibn Tufayl maintains in his conclusion that his narration, far from being a plagiarism, "contains many things that can neither be found in any writings nor heard in any of the current oral narratives." His book derives from books and is not found in any book; it depends on ancient stories and is not the product of any ancient story! This contradiction is the same one that characterizes the protagonist, Hayy, about whom one version maintains that he has a mother and a father and another one claims that he was born by spontaneous generation.

When Ibn Tufayl describes Hayy's account, he no doubt alludes to Moses. However, many are the narratives in diverse

6. In the *Nights*, Shahrazād also refused to listen to her father, who advised her not to set into motion her fate by going to King Shahrayār.

cultures that tell the account of a newborn on the waters, in a forest, or on the top of a mountain. He is usually saved by a shepherd, is breastfed by a woman who is often of a lowly status—sometimes an animal takes care of feeding and caring for him. He grows up in a modest family, whereas in reality he belongs to a royal family.[7] This family saga, based on a double kinship, is reproduced in Ibn Tufayl's story. Hayy has two mothers: the princess who gives birth to him and the gazelle who brings him up and watches over him. He also has two fathers: Yaqzān, who has sired him, and Asāl, who teaches him how to speak and the principles of religious law.

It seems that his uncle, the king of the populated island, behaves according to whim and obeys no other law than that of his own desires and egotism, at least with regard to his sister. His argument for opposing her marriage is that he cannot find someone worthy of her (*kuf'*); in other words, he cannot find anyone equal to *himself*. Thus, the princess should not marry another man.[8] But the sister considers him an "unjust, haughty, stubborn king" and marries Yaqzān, "following a usage authorized by their religion." With this detail, Ibn Tufayl rejects the idea that Hayy was of illegitimate birth. Similarly, by showing the kinship between the princess and Yaqzān, he implies that the latter belongs to the royal family.

The marriage, entered into without the consent of the king, is not made public. Based on a usage accepted by everyone, but not by the king, it remains secret, which in a way compromises its legitimacy. The birth of Hayy must remain secret as well, for it occurs in the space between what is lawful

7. See Rank 1959 and Jung and Kerényi 1980, 46.

8. The indirect reference to Moses may also be taken as a reference to Egypt, to the pharaohs, and to marriage to one's sister.

and what is unlawful. To save the newborn, it must paradoxically be abandoned: its exposure on the waters looks a lot like a trial by ordeal, with the princess leaving the judgment to God. What might seem strange is the fact that her husband, Yaqzān, does not accompany her to the shore; indeed, nothing in the text suggests that she has told him about her decision. Moreover, nothing suggests that he knows he has fathered a child. The father remains lackluster and inconsistent; he is mentioned only briefly in passing, seemingly by accident.

The birth of Hayy thus takes place under difficult circumstances similar to those that occur at the births of heroes. In order for him to have a special destiny, his coming into the world must be unusual, and his upbringing extraordinary. When he grows up and begins to think, he realizes that he is different from other creatures and believes himself to be the only human being on earth. "He stayed like this for a long time, examining the various animal and plant species, walking along the shores of the island, and trying to meet a human being like him, in the same way that he saw in every individual item, animal or vegetable, a great number of fellow members of the species; but he did not find any. Besides, he saw that the sea surrounded the island on all sides, and believed that there was no other land in the world."

During his long solitude, he learns many things, but he remains ignorant concerning his origin. This tallies with the version of a Hayy born without a mother or father, a version that, unlike the other one, denies the sexual dimension. At no time did he think about taking a wife and starting a family. Women are not mentioned at all, even on the island of Salāmān, to which the hero will later travel. The mother appears in the beginning of the story (if we take into account the second version), and the gazelle may be considered a second mother, but otherwise women are completely absent. In one of the manuscripts, we read that on the island where, according to the first version, Hayy is born by spontaneous generation, there is "a tree that, instead of fruits, produces women; [the historian] al-Masʿūdī refers to them by the name 'girls of Waq-wāq.'" However, this passage is manifestly an interpolation: the arboreal women are not mentioned anywhere in the rest of the story.[9]

Insofar as Hayy does not have a genealogy, he has no name and nothing permits us to state that his mother had given him one at birth. It is Ibn Tufayl who names him (basing his argument on Avicenna), whereas Hayy himself does not know his own name, and it is equally unknown to those whom he meets later on. He knows nothing about his parents, unlike the author and reader, who are aware of his story, albeit orally and in an approximate manner because of the two different versions of his birth and the impossibility of knowing which of them is true.

Birth without parents, as a result of spontaneous generation, corresponds to instruction achieved without a teacher. Let us remember that the Latin translation of *Hayy*, published in 1671, bore the title *Philosophus autodidactus*. The hero is all alone; but, as Léon Gauthier points out, "by the combined usage of observation and reasoning he soon comes to discover, all by himself, the highest physical and metaphysical truths."[10] This is all the more remarkable because before his meeting with Asāl he has not learned to speak.

9. Generally speaking, Hayy considers the body to be without value and makes every effort to curb his desires in order to become a pure spirit.

10. See Gauthier 1909, 62. Admirable pages by Ibn Tufayl describe Hayy's efforts "pour arriver à l'évanouissement de la conscience de soi, à l'absorption dans l'intuition pure de [l'Etre] Véritable; et il y réussit

But there is one more thing to be learned—namely, about life in the midst of a human community and the position of the philosopher in the city.[11] The social dimension emerges when Hayy meets Asāl, a character who in the beginning lives on an island neighboring that of the protagonist, one where "one of the solid religions was introduced, derived from one of the ancient prophets[. . .]. It was a religion that expressed all absolute realities through symbols that provided images of those realities and etched them in the soul, such as is the usage in the discourse [addressed to] the vulgar." We note that the discourse changes according to those who receive it: religion (*milla*) is based on parables and symbols that speak to the imagination of the masses, whereas philosophy, aiming at "absolute realities," speaks to the intellect of an enlightened elite.

Asāl and another character, Salāmān, "learned of this religion and embraced it with fervor." But Asāl "searched more thoroughly to penetrate the hidden meaning, to discover the mystic signification, and he was more drawn to allegorical interpretation. Salāmān adhered more to the external meaning and was more inclined to abstain from allegorical interpretation, from independent examination, and from speculation." Nor is that all. Asāl leans toward solitude, whereas Salāmān "was attached to society[. . .]. This difference of opinion was the cause of their separation." Asāl

enfin: [tout] disparut de sa mémoire et de sa pensée [. . .] il ne resta que l'Unique, le Véritable, l'Etre permanent" (to attain the dissipation of self-awareness and absorption in the pure intuition of the [True] Being. He finally succeeded: [everything] disappeared from his memory and thoughts,[. . .] and nothing was left save the Unique, the True, the permanent Being).

11. See Fradkin 1992, 252–56.

then moves to Hayy's island, one that he had heard tell of and assumed was inhabited. His move is in fact an exile reminiscent of that of Hayy upon his birth. Asāl will substitute the company of Hayy for that of Salāmān, as Hayy will substitute Asāl's company for that of the gazelle, long since dead.

The island governed by Salāmān resembles the rich and populated one ruled by Hayy's uncle. However, what especially deserves mention is the analogy between, on the one hand, Yaqzān and Asāl and, on the other, the king and Salāmān. Yaqzān is submissive to the king just as Asāl is subordinate to Salāmān. Both opt for dissimulation and retreat: Yaqzān, afraid of the king's ire, secretly marries the princess; Asāl, hoping to practice allegorical interpretation in utter tranquility, far removed from Salāmān's reprobation, finds refuge on Hayy's island. Various clues reveal Asāl's weakness: he eludes Salāmān and also runs away when he sees Hayy for the first time.

The meeting of the two characters is at first characterized by mistrust, but eventually harmony is to reign between them, especially after Asāl offers Hayy "leftovers from the supplies he had brought with him from the inhabited island." Later he teaches him language. Once they become solid friends, each tells the other his story. "Asāl had no doubt that the traditions of his religious Law concerning God, the powerful and great, his angels, his books, his messengers, the Day of Judgment, his paradise, and the fire of his [hell] were symbols of what Hayy ibn Yaqzān had plainly seen." For his part, Hayy accepts everything that Asāl tells him "about the descriptions of the religious Law" and admits that the prophet "who had written and spread these descriptions was [. . .] sincere in his words and had been sent by his Lord; he trusted him, he believed in his veracity, and testified to his mission."

Nevertheless, Hayy finds two things confusing: "First, why did this messenger most often use allegory when talking to people and in describing the divine world? Why did he abstain from presenting the bare truth?[. . .] Second, why did he stick to these precepts and ritual prescriptions; why did he allow the acquisition of wealth and permit [such] latitude with regard to food, the result being that people gave themselves over to vain occupations and deviated from the truth?" Therefore, he decides to go to Salāmān's island in order to reform its inhabitants. (Here, how can one not be reminded of Don Quixote's "mission"?) Asāl, who knows his world well, tries in vain to dissuade him from doing so. Why does Hayy refuse to listen to him?

To understand his determination (which is somewhat disconcerting), it is perhaps appropriate to tarry for a moment on one detail: when asked by Asāl about his origins, Hayy replies that "he knows neither father nor mother other than the gazelle who raised him." During his period of solitude, he has believed that the gazelle is his mother. Nothing allows us to suppose that he had had any other idea about his ancestry. However, after meeting Asāl, he must have realized without a doubt that he was not the offspring of an animal deprived of reasoning (*ghayr nātiq*). As a consequence, it is only natural for him to desire to identify his parents and make the effort to find them. In similar stories, the abandoned child grows up in a new family but sooner or later returns to his real parents (Rank 1959, 89). Hayy will never meet his own parents, something that does not seem to arouse his curiosity; at least, he has never been bothered by it.[12] We might suggest that

12. After the gazelle dies, Hayy dissects its body in search of the secret of life—in other words, his own secret.

in his wish to remain unique he does not concern himself about his parents. However, we can also interpret his move to Salāmān's island as a quest for his origins.

Be that as it may, "full of compassion for Mankind and fervently desiring to bring it salvation, he hatched the plan to go to them, to expose the clear and evident truth to them[. . .]. But he had barely risen above the exoteric meaning so as to tackle certain [truths] that conflicted with their prejudices when they began to withdraw from him: their souls were disgusted by the [doctrines] that he brought them, and they grew annoyed with him in their hearts." Let us point out that he has only spoken to the *murīdūn*, a privileged group of disciples. That is because Asāl has warned him "that this group of men prevailed over everyone else as far as intelligence and perceptiveness were concerned, and that if he did not succeed in teaching them, he would be even less successful in teaching the masses." Yet even though his discourse sows discord in people's minds, Hayy is not persecuted. The conflict remains concealed and does not end in violent confrontation. The disciples look "pleasantly upon him out of courtesy toward a foreigner and out of respect for their friend Asāl." In other words, had he not been a foreigner and a protégé of Asāl, he would have experienced a different fate.

If they had accepted his teaching, he would probably have stayed among them permanently. But, having failed to accomplish the mission he had taken upon himself,[13] he "went to Salāmān and his companions, apologized for the speeches he had made before them, and recanted. He declared to them that he would thenceforth think like them; their norms would

13. In a sense, he accomplishes a heroic act when, by himself, he succeeds in acquiring his overall knowledge.

be his as well. He advised them strictly to observe the limits of divine law and its external practices and to delve as little as possible into things that did not concern them." Now, had he really shared their way of thinking, he would never have left them. Though not threatened openly, he no doubt felt that a danger was hovering over him. But his retraction—and here one is reminded of that of Don Quixote on his deathbed—is essentially the result of his conviction that those to whom he has spoken are not qualified to receive wisdom's secrets, "that to speak to them about the pure truth was a vain thing," and, moreover, "that most of them may be ranked with animals deprived of reasoning." This means that while on Salāmān's island, Hayy remains as he was on his own island: the sole human being among beasts. But there is a difference in proportion: on his island Hayy is the undisputed and unrivaled master of the animals, whereas on Salāmān's island he is unable to impose his domination.

His departure constitutes a second exile, one that is in every respect similar to the first, which he experienced when he was born. As we notice, the end is dramatic and disturbing, just as was the beginning. At the outset, an unwanted child is placed in a chest and entrusted to the waves; at the end, a philosopher who appears to be an intruder can do nothing else but take to the sea again and return to his island. There are so many islands in this story, close to one another but irrevocably separated—islands that are secluded and self-sufficient, completely cut off. Hayy's island does not suit Salāmān, nor does Salāmān's island suit Hayy. Just as the king prevents his sister from getting married because he can find no suitor worthy of her, so does Salāmān reject philosophy because he does not find it compatible with religious law. However, a compromise is reached on Hayy's island, which also becomes Asāl's.

When the name "Ibn Tufayl" is mentioned, the Arabic reader links it more or less to the word *tifl* (child) and to the word *tufaylī* (intruder, parasite, and sponger[14]). Hayy is an intruder, both when he comes into this world without having been asked and when he goes to Salāmān's island to spread a teaching that no one wants to hear. In both cases, he creates a scandal, and his punishment is exile.

He certainly addresses the disciples orally. Thanks to Asāl, Hayy learns language, but he does not seem to have learned how to write. At no time does he concern himself with books. There is no mention of the act of writing in his narratives to the *murīdūn* (moreover, there is no explicit indication that the religion of the inhabited island is derived from a book, even if incidental reference is made to revealed books). On the other hand, Ibn Tufayl delivers his teaching through writing and, to avert suspicion of meddling, resorts to a traditional process, pretending to have written *Hayy ibn Yaqzān* only in order to satisfy the request of a correspondent who wants to learn about Avicenna's philosophy: "You have asked me, generous, sincere, devoted brother [. . .] to reveal to you what I can of the secrets of the enlightening philosophy handed down by the master [. . .] Ibn Sīnā."

Even though Ibn Tufayl has not written on his own initiative, he still finds himself incapable of getting rid of a certain anxiety: he has revealed what should have remained hidden. He acknowledges this in the conclusion to his book: "By publishing it, we have deviated from the code of conduct followed by our virtuous ancestors who jealously kept such

14. *Tufayl*, *tifl*, and *tufaylī*: these three words have the same root in Arabic.

a matter secret and were miserly about sharing it." Like his hero, who apologizes to Asāl's companions, Ibn Tufayl apologizes to his brothers, namely philosophers: "As for me, I beg my brothers who will read this book to accept my apologies for the liberties I have taken in the exposition and my lack of rigor in the demonstration." As we have already seen, Ibn Tufayl stressed the virtuous predecessors whom he claims to cite, but now he admits to having published what they never said. Thus, the ancestors either speak or do not; or, should one prefer, we might say that there is that which is said and that which remains tacit. In this sense, their divergence concerning Hayy's birth remains superficial, destined to conceal knowledge from the common people.

Beside the ancestors, Ibn Tufayl cites mystics and philosophers who have preceded him. In the pages that he devotes to them, he stresses the contradiction that they experience between their desire to speak and their sense that they should remain silent. The ecstatic state lived by the mystic is "so extraordinary that language cannot describe it, nor can speech account for it," but he who "has reached one of these levels cannot keep silent about it or hide its secret: he is consumed by an emotion, an ardor, an exuberance, and a joy that compel him to convey the secret of that state in an approximate and vague manner." Generally speaking, Ibn Tufayl's speech on philosophers is a discourse about their ways of writing and how they express their thoughts (see Mallet 1997). What he has to say about them is focused on the fundamental duality that characterizes them, on their singular art of combining confession and silence. Thus, Ibn Bājjāh's style is confused and awkward: "Most of his works lack polish and are abbreviated in the end." One cannot exclude the possibility that Ibn Tufayl is here suggesting that Ibn Bājjāh's text is chaotic by design (Strauss 1988, 98–99). Al-Fārābī, adds Ibn Tufayl, contradicts himself from one book to the next when he discusses the fate of souls after death. As for al-Ghazālī, "inasmuch as he addresses the masses, he is reticent in one place and speaks freely in another; accuses certain opinions of infidelity, then declares them lawful." As for Avicenna's *Shifā'*, it cannot be fully understood if we limit ourselves to the "exoteric meaning, without searching for its profound esoteric meaning."

Ibn Tufayl scrupulously practiced this art of writing. He certainly expressed a wisdom that should have remained hidden, but he did it in an indirect way, behind a veil, as he puts it—in such a way that only those who are equipped to understand it will be able to uncover its secrets. In a word, what he has revealed will remain a secret between him and his brothers: "But we have taken care to cover the secrets that we entrust to these few pages with a light veil, which will promptly be pierced by those worthy of doing so but will remain impenetrably opaque to anyone unworthy of progressing beyond it." His book is thus composed of two books: one, which is open, for the masses; and the other, which is closed, for philosophers. We should recall that he is addressing a disciple who fervently wishes to learn and that their relationship is built upon trust. The correspondent, this "generous and sincere brother," is trustworthy and will undoubtedly keep the secrets with all necessary diligence, revealing them only to those ready to receive them. Those without these qualities do not deserve to read *Hayy*, and, in any event, their reading will not allow them to decipher the secrets contained within the book.

This relationship between the author and a familiar and trustworthy person is analogous to that which links Hayy to the gazelle and later to Asāl. The teaching of Ibn Tufayl will not reach beyond a small, intimate circle, which brings us back to the story's beginning, to the persecuted princess heading to the shore at nightfall to cast off her son, accompanied only by "servants and trustworthy friends," a limited group that is party to a secret and will never reveal it.

6 The Hostile Eye

One editor has noted that certain passages of Ibn Hazm's *Tawq al–hamāmah* (*The Dove's Neck-Ring*) are so daring that he almost expurgated them (Makki 1980, 10).[1] But what was he afraid of? For no voice had been raised to condemn the *Neck-Ring* in its earlier editions or to express the least reservation regarding its content. Putting forward as justification the respect owed to the heritage, the editor finally decided to publish the book in its entirety. But in his reticence, which does not seem to be a mere rhetorical precaution, he paradoxically invites us to consider *The Dove's Neck-Ring* as a reprehensible book. The reader is thus invited to find the suspect passages and serve against his will as a censor (or a voyeur). However, how are we to recognize the virtually reprehensible passages? What criteria should we use in order to separate the chaff from the wheat?

Ibn Hazm was aware of the novelty of his venture. He dissociated himself from the love stories of the desert dwellers, for whom he had contempt: "Excuse me from bringing up the tales of the Bedouins and the ancients, for their ways

1. *Translators' note*: Here we refer the reader to *The Dove's Neck-Ring, about Love and Lovers*, translated by A. R. Nykl from the unique manuscript in the University of Leiden (Ibn Hazm 1931).

are different from ours." The love he describes occurs against the backdrop of the city of Córdoba, with its neighborhoods, alleys, bridges, houses, and shops. Furthermore—all the while conforming to the rules of traditional poetic style—he distances himself from the hyperbole and bombast of erotic poetry. Annoyed by poems that present the man in love as an emaciated anorexic and an inveterate insomniac, he declares that as far as he is concerned, he has "confined [myself] in this treatise [of mine] to well-known truths beside which nothing can exist at all."

Let us remember that *The Dove's Neck-Ring* is composed of thirty chapters, each of which defines some aspect of love: exchanges of letters, the messenger, the union, fidelity, betrayal, separation, and so on. Some general considerations are demonstrated by anecdotes as well as by poems authored by Ibn Hazm himself. It appears to me that the originality and audacity of the book are essentially exemplified by its anecdotes, or at least by some of them. Here is one anecdote upon which, for some obscure reason, I have fixed my choice, revolving around a declaration of love:

> I know a slave-girl who fell passionately in love with a young man, son of a chief, but he knew nothing about it. As a consequence, her grief grew; her sorrow was endless, until she became sick on account of her love of him. But, with the indifference of youth, he did not realize it. Modesty prevented her from telling him about her feelings, for she was a perfect virgin, added to which was her respect for him [which prevented her] from initiating a conversation with him about something where she did not know if it would meet with his approval. When this situation continued and the certainty of it was growing (in her), she complained about it to a woman, one who was very wise in her opinions and whom she trusted because she had

> been in charge of her education (upbringing). The latter said: "Make allusion to him in poetry." The girl did so time and again, but he still paid no attention, even though he was endowed with a subtle mind and intelligent. He did not realize (she was in love), something that might have inclined him to inquire into the meaning of words.

What happens next is unexpected and might shock certain readers (but which, one wonders?). Before we tell it, let us point out that this anecdote illustrates an idea that is dear to Ibn Hazm, the close complicity that exists between women from the moment that a love affair is involved.[2] The young girl, unable to bear the weight of her secret alone and incapable of opening up to the young man whom she loves, turns to the woman who has raised her and still functions as both mother and confidante. Apparently initiated into the games of love, the latter does not discourage the girl and indeed advises her to recite poems to the beloved one—poetry being, according to Ibn Hazm, an indirect way of declaring one's love. Poems charm and inspire love (Are they not, according to a certain archaic belief, the breath of demons?). However, the young man remains indifferent to the solicitation of the poems, to the love call. Literature having no hold over him, he fails to interpret the signs correctly—it is true that he is "still under the power of childhood."

2. "I have never known anyone more favorable in love than women. They have, in order to keep secrets, to mutually confide the dissimulation, to agree to veil it when they discover it, something that does not exist among men. I have never seen women reveal the secret of those in love without drawing hatred from the other, a contempt and condemnation that is uttered in unison."

After trying in vain to attract the young man's attention by reciting poetry, the girl resorts to a unique way of declaring her love:

> Her patience was gone, and her heart was so oppressed that she lost all control over herself during a tête-à-tête she had with him one night all alone. She was God-fearing, restrained, and self-possessed, far removed from the very idea of doing anything wrong. When the time came for her departure, she rushed over to him and kissed him on the mouth. Then, without saying a word, she turned around and walked away, swaying her body proudly and coquettishly[. . .]. He was dumbfounded, completely taken aback[. . .]. The moment she disappeared from his sight, he fell into perdition's net. A violent fire was kindled in his heart, and he began to heave deep sighs. His fears began to pile up on each other; his anxiety grew, and his sleeplessness was prolonged. That night he could not sleep a wink. That was the start of a longtime love between them until separation caused it to end.

By her behavior, the girl has transgressed a rule that the text suggests without mentioning it explicitly: the initiative of the declaration of love is the responsibility of the man, not the woman. Ibn Rashīq al-Qayrawānī, a contemporary of Ibn Hazm, expresses it clearly in his book of poetic criticism, *Al-ʻUmdah fī mahāsin al-shiʻr wa adabihi wa naqdihi* (The mainstay concerning poetry's embellishments, correct usage, and criticism): "The custom among Arabs is that the poet is responsible for expressing gallant sentiments and playing the role of the suffering lover. With non-Arabs (ʻAjam) it is the opposite. They have the custom of attributing the initiative to the woman: it is up to her to desire and speak. This proves the nobility of the nature of the Arabs."

The young girl has behaved like a non-Arab, something that she seems to be, as it were, for she is a slave (*jāriyah*). But she does not settle simply for speaking out by reciting verses but goes even further by kissing the young man and thereby breaking yet another rule: the initiative for the first kiss belongs to the man and him alone. She is thus guilty of a double transgression (in both cases, the mouth is involved). For a woman to usurp a power attributed to men is scandalous; in such a situation, there is a disruption of the roles allotted to each of the sexes. In this upside-down world, the female has taken over the male's role. This infringement of male prerogative must have horrified Ibn Rashīq al-Qayrawānī, who, full of hatred for the non-Arab woman though he may have been, would scarcely go so far as to think her capable of initiating a passionate kiss.

To my knowledge, there is no precedent in either poetry or narrative for reporting such a deed. However, let us recall two memorable kisses. The first is in the story of Lancelot: Queen Guinevere kisses Lancelot; it is she who takes the first step, it must be said, but she obeys a suggestion by Galehaut, a friend of the knight. Thus, one can say that male privilege remains intact. The second kiss, no doubt even more famous, is described in canto V of Dante's *Inferno*. Paolo and Francesca, while indeed reading the story of Lancelot and Guinevere, discover their own passions. But it is Paolo who initiates the kiss. As Francesca tells Dante,

> [L]a bocca mi basciò tutto tremante.
> Galeotto fu 'l libro e chi lo scrisse:
> Quel giorno più non vi leggemmo avante.

[And trembling, he kissed me on the mouth.
Galehaut was at once the book and he who wrote it:
Nor did we that day read any further.][3]

In Ibn Hazm's story, the kiss is not suggested to the young girl by her confidante, nor is it inspired by a literary model, whether in poetry or in book form. It is a matter of a sudden, unpremeditated impulse with uncertain consequences—a risky gamble, which has miraculously been won. The young man, unmoved at first by the poetic prompting, gives in to the kiss that awakens his passion and makes him come to himself. All things considered, it is a savage and violent story, one in which Ibn Hazm, who is clearly aware of this, obviously sees "one of the Devil's snares and strange causes in love which can only be resisted by one to whom protection is granted by God, Most High and Exalted."

The Dove's Neck-Ring is preserved for us thanks to a unique manuscript, and it is rather curious that such an important work has been preserved in only a single copy, one made three centuries after Ibn Hazm's death! However, most troubling is the fact that the transcriber, at the end of the book, declares that he has deleted "most of the poems so as to leave only the best." This mutilation of the text is perhaps

3. *Translators' note*: Dante's *Inferno*, canto V, lines 136–38, our translation. This is one of the most famous passages in Dante Alighieri's *Divine Comedy*. Many of the published translations of the *Inferno* are accompanied by a note explaining who Galeotto (Galehot, Galehaut) is and the literary antecedents of this seductive moment between Paolo and Francesca, as well as the fact that "Galeotto" is not only the name of this person, but also in Italian means, among other things, "pimp," "procurer," and "panderer."

not very serious for our lazy minds: we generally skip verses that accompany texts in prose (although it is certainly a mistake for us to do so). But some people have also suspected this copyist of also suppressing texts in prose, anecdotes or statements about love that may not have suited his taste or that he may have found too brazen. In any case, the book we now read is not exactly the one that Ibn Hazm wrote.

The shadow of censorship thus looms over *The Neck-Ring*. Moreover, the author himself has yielded to self-censorship: what he has written differs from what he could have written. He frequently specifies that there are things he either does not want to say or cannot say and that he has not recorded everything he knows about love. What is the origin of this knowledge that he refuses to disclose even in part? The secluded space of the women's quarters. Women had introduced him to the secrets of love; he had been raised by them and, as a preadolescent, had lived exclusively in their midst: "From a long time ago, I was a witness among women, and I learned more about their secrets than anyone else. After all, they had raised me on their bosoms, and I grew up in their good hands. I knew only them.[. . .] They taught me the Qur'ān, fed me poetry, and shaped my writing. As my intelligence took its first steps in early childhood, I had no other task, nor was my mind trapped by any toils other than to find out what makes them act and to investigate what lives they have lived, then to make that my own."

If he remains silent concerning part of what he had learned from women, it is so as not to stir up guilty desires in the reader: "I continued to investigate stories about women, discovering their secrets. They realized that my custom was discretion, so that they kept telling me about the most profoundly discreet of their affairs. Were I not mindful of the need not to divulge shameful things, from which I pray for

God's protection, I would be talking now about their alertness to evil and their astuteness with regard to it, marvelous things which would astonish men of intelligence."

Ibn Hazm thus received a double upbringing, both feminine and masculine. The first coincides with his childhood and consists of three themes: the Qur'ān, poetry, and the secrets of love. That period of formation was mainly oral (although women did teach him to write). The masculine formation, which began only at adolescence, was based on *virile* subjects, including theology, a subject in which Ibn Hazm distinguished himself.

Women as well as men recount the many anecdotes that are narrated in *The Neck-Ring*, even if the former's contribution is relatively less important. Sometimes the anecdotes are the author's personal memories, tales of his loves. On occasion, he reveals his secrets, as when he announces that the first woman he fell in love with was a blonde and that he has "never cared for black hair since." This arouses the suspicion that, in certain anecdotes, he has attributed his own experiences to other characters. Who knows? He may be the young man kissed by the slave girl.

To reiterate, *The Neck-Ring* would have been different had Ibn Hazm recorded everything that women taught him. It is a book fraught with what is not told, with feminine secrets that remain veiled. Besides, the lover, as depicted by Ibn Hazm, is more often than not a secretive being, withdrawn into himself, who makes every effort not to reveal his love. However, he is surrounded by people who are watching him and waiting for the slightest hint that might betray his feelings. Three antagonists of the author are to be feared: the censor (*'ādhil*), the spy (*raqīb*), and the informer (*wāshī*). To love is to dissimulate, to try to mislead—also to feel guilty about violating a taboo. Ibn Hazm describes a universe in which guards and chaperones are everywhere. The spy is always on the prowl.

Let us note that Ibn Hazm presents his book as the result of the suggestion of a friend who had asked him to write it. (This may be true, but we might also take it as an affectation, an opening protocol well established by tradition.) In composing his book, Ibn Hazm has responded to a solicitation, a wish; in other words, the initiative does not come from him. The initiative again! He has yielded to a request, a little bit like the young man in our story who responds to the kiss. We get the impression that Ibn Hazm is trying to blame the act of writing the book on the anonymous commissioner; at the very least, he tries to mitigate his responsibility by implying that he wrote it in spite of himself, under friendly pressure that is certainly analogous to the erotic pressure the young man was subjected to.

Ibn Hazm's tone, so free, abruptly changes in the last two chapters, entitled "The Ugliness of Sin" and "Fullness of Abstinence." It becomes moralizing and severe. We are far removed from the earlier chapter where he boasted: "I trod upon Caliphs' rugs; I sat in kings' councils. I have never noticed there anything that compares with the reverent fear that the lover shows toward his loved one. I have seen victors holding the life of an enemy chief at their mercy[. . .], but I have never seen more intense exultation, more radiant joy, than that shown by a lover who is assured of the heart of his loved one, convinced of the liking that one has for him and the affection one brings him." The last chapter of the *Neck-Ring* ends abruptly with a long poem consisting of an exhortation in favor of abstinence. In it we can detect a malaise, and we get the impression that Ibn Hazm has reached a dead end. Specifically, one of his characters, upon entering an alley, "saw a young woman standing, her face unveiled, who said to him: 'Hey you! This is an impasse. We cannot get out of it.'"

Ibn Hazm fears reprobation from some of his readers: "I know that certain zealots will condemn me for having written such a book." To defend himself, he feels compelled to declare that he has never acted immorally or shamefully: "I swear to God that I have never undressed to commit a forbidden sexual act." What does this suggest, if not that he feels the spying eye leveled at him? The censor is observing the lover and the author as well. Taking everything into account, love and writing are one and the same thing. Both arouse the same mistrust.

Not only does Ibn Hazm fear his readers' reactions, but he also feels watched over by the two angels who are charged with taking note of the good and bad actions of man: "For me, I ask the Almighty God for forgiveness for what the two angels will write down, for what they will have to record about this book, and for the topic with which it deals." Unlike the mutilated copy available to us, the celestial copy of the book, compiled by the two angels, is complete.

7 Al-Mu'tamid's *Dahr*

In the eyes of many of his readers, al-Mu'tamid ibn 'Abbād owes much to his defeat at the hands of the Almoravids and his exile in faraway Aghmāt. His removal from office, a supreme misfortune, proved to be a boon. He may have lost his kingdom, but he also gained immortality and a prized place in people's memories. His misfortune has become a beautiful story, told and listened to with sympathy and compassion. What makes him even more touching is the impression that he was the victim of a sudden change of fate: as the greatest prince in Andalusia, he was at the height of his power when his fall occurred. Dispossessed of his kingdom, he became a beggar king.

One is inclined to compare him to his father, al-Mu'tadid, who consolidated the 'Abbadid dynasty. But al-Mu'tadid died at the height of his glory. His military undertakings were crowned with success; he won resounding victories—as Ibn al-Khatīb notes with admiration—while remaining in his palace, comfortably seated on his throne. He thus acted from afar, without exerting himself—in a sense without moving, something that endowed him with a quasi-divine power. As is only fitting, he was also generous, surrounding himself with poets and not averse to writing doggerel of his own on occasion. Nevertheless, even as chroniclers praise his energy, they also denounce his ferocity, although they were careful not to go into too much detail on the subject. Nor were his family members spared his cruelty. Did he not kill one of his children with his own hands? This does not make for a good story; in fact, it is almost beyond words. The poet Ibn al-Labbāna declares modestly that, with regard to certain of al-Muʻtadid's actions, it is better to pass over them in silence. All in all, and despite the unspeakable things of which this prince was guilty, luck continued to favor him.

When speaking of al-Muʻtadid, chroniclers inevitably think of his son, the unfortunate al-Muʻtamid. The latter apparently did not choose to be the hero of a wonderful story, a tear-jerking narrative. What he did want was to be remembered as a king who had perpetuated his father's lofty deeds, someone who was generous, brave in battle, praised by poets—in brief, someone who fit the image one finds in panegyric poems. Al-Muʻtadid was his model, and one can affirm that for most of his reign he was a worthy successor to his father. However, he did not manage to emulate him to the bitter end and finished up squandering his patrimony. It must be said that even when his father was still alive, there were signs that al-Muʻtamid was incapable of being his father's equal and living up to his success. Having failed to secure the defense of Malaga against the troops of Badis ibn Habbūs, he was forced to take refuge in Ronda, where for a time he lived in fear of his father's wrath. This was a test, a period of exile that prefigures his exile in Aghmāt. He spent his time writing poems, among which is the long *rā'iyya* (poem rhyming on *r*) addressed to his father in the hope that the latter would pardon him and restore him to grace. Poems such as this one are harbingers of those that he would later write far away from Andalusia.

How did he become a beggar king? The exile poems are an attempt to answer this question. Here it is important to note that, contrary to what happens to the heroes of Greek tragedy, at no time does he display a sense of guilt. Historians claim that he made many errors of judgment and that through his tortuous strategies he contributed to the fall of Toledo, an event that was all too painfully identified as a precursor to the end of Muslim dominance in the Iberian Peninsula. However, it is not on that level that he considers things in his poems: he does not feel responsible for what has happened to him. He has defended his kingdom against the Almoravids, fought to the end, and even nearly been killed during the siege of Seville. His courage and energy are not in question. Yet the result is evident: he has lost everything. As he has no reason to blame himself for anything, he attributes it all to a supernatural force, destiny (*dahr*), a notion that recurs frequently in his poems, in addition to others from the same semantic field: luck (*hazz*), God's immutable judgment (*aqdār*), and nights (*layālī*).

Dahr is presented as al-Mu'tamid's principal enemy. However, it has also been his ally, even subject to his orders. But now here it is, turning against him and betraying him: "When you were in charge of it, your *dahr* was under your orders, but now it has rendered you docile and submissive" (*Dīwān* 2002, n.p.).

What al-Mu'tamid is unable to forgive himself for is that he had previously trusted this power, which by its very nature is capricious and inconstant: "Whoever keeps *dahr* company will certainly see it change."

All things considered, the vicissitudes of *dahr* are analogous to the shifting alliances in relations between the various actors in the political life of Spain. Yesterday's ally will tomorrow be transformed into a fierce adversary, a friend will suddenly become an enemy, and an enemy a friend. One need only recall al-Mu'tamid's relationship with his vizier Ibn

'Ammār and, on another level, with Yūsuf ibn Tāshfīn and Alfonso VI. The variations of *dahr* are a perfect reflection of the vicissitudes of political life in Spain and the Maghrib.

Nonetheless, Mu'tamid did bestow an absolute trust on *dahr*. He tried to make good use of it and not to thwart it. Before acting, he would carefully probe his intentions through recourse to an astrologer's observations. On the night before the battle of al-Zallāqa, the astrologer had his say and made no mistakes in his calculations. However, later his prophecies proved to be false, and so, once Seville was besieged, he fled. Al-Mu'tamid poked fun at him in one of his poems: "What you have promised has turned into its opposite."

To lose everything is to give everything back. Here one can observe a traditional motif: *dahr* always takes back what it has granted: "Every time it gives a precious thing, it snatches it away."

This is a trait that shows *dahr*'s treachery, baseness, and iniquity (*lu'm*). A well-bred man does not take back what he has given. However, once again, if one examines the political context of the time, one will certainly notice the coincidence between this motif and the relationship between a prince and his entourage. After all, at one time or another, which Andalusian king did not strip his viziers of all their possessions (of everything he had given them)?

If *dahr* is subject to change, it is also susceptible to growing soft, shifting, and going off on another tack. In hard times, there always remains a hope that it might change its mood. But al-Mu'tamid scarcely embraces this hope; he knows it will be in vain. He will not recover his kingdom; *dahr* will not even grant him the favor of a glance. But he continues to contemplate the sky and to question the flight patterns of birds, those messengers of the other world. Indeed, *dahr* has some minor pleasures in store for him. Thus, one of his wives joins him in Aghmāt, a piece of good fortune that is announced to him by the cawing of crows! Signs of destiny are not certain: crows, traditionally bad omens, for once are bearers of glad tidings. Al-Mu'tamid praises them and declares in gratitude that he will never again call them "one-eyed" (*a'war*), given that, of course, a one-eyed person is an evil omen and that "*al-a'war*" is a name used for a crow. One can also cite the poem in which he describes a flock of pigeons (*qatā*) flying free while he himself is in chains and unable to move about. They represent precisely the things of which he is deprived—namely, elevation and domination. He envies them their freedom and ease of movement, even as he admits—a fine example of apophasis—that he feels no envy toward them.

A leitmotif in his poems is the parallel that he establishes between his past glory and present misery. He recalls his palaces in Seville and the splendors of yore, but then he immediately laments the spectacle of his misfortune and the fact that his daughter has been reduced to spinning wool for one of his former servants. He consoles himself by noting that he is not the first person upon whom such a trial has been imposed; many a king before him has been betrayed by *dahr* (the theme of the "fallen prince"). He also provides a melancholy invocation of the inevitability of death and the vanity of human ventures (*vanitas vanitatum*). But what seems to irritate him the most is that he can no longer bestow any gifts. Power can be equated with the ability to give generously and thus to assure oneself of other people's obeisance. Generosity is not a quality of the soul, as poets claim, but rather a means of dominance. No longer being able to give implies no longer having power. Nevertheless, he continues to deceive himself by acting as if he were still able to display largesse. In Tangier, he gives thirty gold pieces to the poet Hursī, thus depriving himself of what he has left in order to maintain the illusion that he is still a king. Once the other poets of the city get wind of this act of generosity, they come to him, clamoring for money from the one who has lost everything—beggars asking for alms from a beggar, a situation that is not entirely devoid of humor. In Aghmāt, he gives twenty gold pieces to the poet Ibn al-Labbāna, who thoughtfully refuses them. Although al-Muʻtamid appreciates this tactful gesture, he is nevertheless offended, for he sees reflected in it his loss of power. It might also be appropriate to interpret in this same sense the many poems in which he speaks about his chains (*qayd*). To be in chains is to be immobilized, but also no longer able to give. The hand of al-Muʻtamid is tied not by greed, but by destitution; he is unable to open it.[1]

It is worth noting that he adopts two different attitudes, depending on whether he is invoking *dahr* or Allah. We know that the ambiguity attached to the concept of *dahr* has aroused considerable theological debate, focused on a pronouncement attributed to the Prophet: "Do not insult *dahr*, for Allah is *dahr*." This idea is directed, needless to say, against the pre-Islamic belief that considers *dahr* to be responsible for what happens in the world. But, despite this warning, poets have still treated *dahr* harshly. Al-Muʻtamid himself blames *dahr* and heaps reproaches on it. He certainly acknowledges its superiority, but, in his indignation at its conduct and in the vague hope of taking revenge, he can at least denounce it. However, when he invokes Allah, his tone changes, as in these two verses in which he converses with his wife, Iʻtimād:

1. One recognizes the Qur'ānic verse that orders one to be neither greedy nor prodigal: "You shall not keep your hand stingily tied to your neck, nor shall you foolishly open it up" (17:29)

She says: We have fallen here into degradation, Lord;
where is our dignity?
I replied to her: Here is where our God has led us.

Neither one of them could go any further, for that would have meant opposing divine will. The only possible response is to lay down one's arms and accept what cannot be challenged. If al-Mu'tamid cannot contend with God, he can at least do so with *dahr.* In other words, he challenges *dahr* but surrenders to God. Something that helps explain the twin themes that characterize his poems: revolt and submission.

Although he has lost everything, he still has poetry, and it is there that he finds his salvation. Poets such as Ibn al-Labbāna and Ibn Hamdīs visit him or send him verses. In the East as in the West, people feel sorry for him and sympathize with his misfortune; they narrate his story and recite his poems: "The news of your captivity has spread everywhere and has draped many regions of the earth with profound emotion."

The world is watching him; he has become an object of contemplation, of meditation. He is needlessly saddled with a pathetic life on earth but realizes that he is already firmly ensconced in the afterlife, in immortality; his destiny will be exceptional. He is definitively anchored in man's memory, so what is the point of staying alive? Besides, he is actually already dead: Does he not push complacency to the extent of composing, in epitaph form, a poem in which he creates his own eulogy? Thus, he will continue to speak after death; indeed, he will continue to live. This is to be his bitter revenge on *dahr.*

8 The Singing of the Jinns

For many readers, the desert is linked to *Al-Muʿallaqāt* (The suspended poems), the pre-Islamic odes that open in a bedouin context with a description of an abandoned camp. The beloved is no longer present, presumably gone with her people in search of new pastures to graze their flocks. Erased by the wind and rain and buried under the sand, the camp has been reduced to a few tracks and constitutes little more than a desolate and melancholy landscape.

The desert as described in *Al-Muʿallaqāt* does not seem very disturbing. However, other poems of the same period mention formidable lands "where the traveler could die (*baydāʾ*)." One must not linger there. In spite of appearances, they are far from uninhabited: their population consists of wild animals and people who, like the bandit poets (*saʿālīk*), have cut all ties with their tribes. The desert is the place of exile for those who, having disregarded the rules of the community, were repudiated by their own people and condemned to a life of wandering. A metamorphosis takes place in them, and they are reduced to the level of animals. In a famous poem, the bandit poet al-Shanfarā announces to his people that he is leaving them to join a new family, one of wolves and hyenas.

Other creatures that are supernatural or monstrous loom in these baneful places. Venturing there, the traveler treads on the territory of demons and is overcome by a sense of terror. In *Murūj al-dhahab wa maʿādin al-jawāhir* (*Meadows of Gold and Mines of Gems*),[1] the historian al-Masʿūdī, who is often compared to Herodotus, has cataloged the fiendish beings that haunt the desert. He writes of mysterious voices that can be heard, issuing from invisible beings, the *hawātif* (plural of *hātif*): "The principal function of a *hātif* is to create a voice whose sound can be heard without one's discovering the body that made it." On that list we also find the *shiqq*, or demon, "half of whose body has a human form. One comes upon them when one is traveling and entirely isolated." In it we also find the ghouls "that choose ruins and deserts for refuge." They "appear to travelers, at night and at an hour when no one is up and about any longer. Travelers take them for companions and follow them, but the demons mislead them and make them lose their way." The female ghoul appears in different forms in solitary places, but despite these metamorphoses she seems to have a physical characteristic that makes her recognizable: "The Arabs claim [. . .] that the two feet of the female ghoul are donkey's hooves." At night she lights fires to attract travelers. To avoid succumbing to her call, one would recite this incantation: "O monster with donkey's feet, bray as much as you like, we will leave neither the plain nor the road we are following."

She would then run away "into the depths of the valleys and atop the mountain peaks." However, there were also those people, like the bandit poet Ta'abbata Sharran, who were not afraid to meet her and took her as a wife:

> At dawn, the ghoul came to me to become my bride: "O my companion," I told her, "how frightful you look!"

1. Translated from the Arabic by Aloys Sprenger (al-Masʿūdī 1841).

> So I asked favors of her, and she prostrated herself in front of me and by a complete transformation assumed features now unrecognizable.
>
> If someone asks me who my partner is, I shall answer that she had established her home in the folds of the desert sands.

The ghoul takes after both Man and Beast. In this connection, al-Mas'ūdī remarks that "ghouls are animals belonging to a class absolutely apart from other species, one of hideous shape and eluding the common laws of nature. As their external form and instincts isolate them from all beings, they search for the wildest solitudes and are happy only in the wilderness." Is it mere coincidence that we have linked the female ghoul, which eschews the common laws of nature, to Ta'abbata Sharran, who flees the communal laws of the tribe?

Did al-Mas'ūdī believe these stories? He is extremely careful, like Herodotus taking the precaution on each occasion to acknowledge his references—primarily poets, but also anonymous sources. He makes use of phrases such as "the Arabs say" and "According to a certain number of authors." He occasionally apologizes for telling stories that might seem weird or incredible. Let us not forget that he is addressing city dwellers, for whom such phenomena must seem remote in both space and time. So he tries to explain them rationally, albeit without personally involving himself:

> A certain number of authors believe that everything the Arabs have said about this subject was the product of an imagination overly stimulated by solitude in plains, by isolation in valleys, by treks across vast steppes and the wildest of deserts. They say, in fact, that, when a man finds

> himself alone in such places, he gives himself over to dark reveries that spawn anxiety and fear. Under these conditions, his heart easily opens up to superstitious beliefs and apprehensions that bring disorder to his soul, ever susceptible to dark forebodings. They make him hear mysterious voices and see ghosts; they fill him with the fear of the extraordinary beings that a troubled brain creates.[. . .] As a result, he is prepared to believe in the authenticity of tales that he has been told regarding the voices of the *hawātif* and jinns.

Al-Mas'ūdī seems to bring about a disenchantment with the desert by ridding it of its supernatural population. But, once again, this is possible only from an urban perspective that boasts of its rationalism. Yet the fact remains that for him the desert is still a place of deceptive appearances, appalling mirages, and death disguised as life. Consider this beautiful passage describing a sculpture shaped by jinns, near the grave of the poet Hātim al-Tā'ī:

> To the right of the grave there are four young girls sculpted in stone; to the left, four others of the same kind, all of them with disheveled hair and positioned by the tomb like mourners. No one has ever seen anything comparable to the whiteness of their bodies and the beauty of their faces. They have been fashioned by the jinns themselves[. . .]. People passing by this place and looking at these young girls are often struck by their beauty. Such is their admiration that they stray from their way in order to contemplate them at their leisure. However once they draw closer, they realize that they are just sculptures.

In an inhospitable place, we find the grave of a poet whose generosity has become proverbial. The jinns seem to regret his disappearance: at night their voices are raised "in pitiful tones." However, these masters of illusion are able neither to resuscitate nor to bring to life the statues they have fashioned in his honor.

9 Portrait of the Miser as a Hero

Misers do not believe at all in a future life; the present is everything to them.

—Honoré de Balzac,
Eugénie Grandet

Al-Jāhiz had read "all the books," but without having become of "weary flesh."[1] It is believed that he established a theological school, whose name was derived from his own, the Jāhiziyya; it is also believed that he was its sole member. It could not have been otherwise. Al-Jāhiz was unique, and he occupies an exceptional place in Arabic literature. *Kitāb al-bukhala'* (*The Book of Misers* [al-Jāhiz 2000]), in an excellent [French] translation by Charles Pellat (al-Jāhiz 1997), provides resounding proof of this.

In the preface, al-Jāhiz mentions one of his works that has not come down to us, *Tasnīf hiyal al-lusūs* (The classification of the tricks of thieves). This mention is probably not gratuitous: it demands that *The Book of Misers* be read as an inventory of misers' strategies, they being people constantly on the alert and for whom others are real or potential

1. Compare Mallarmé's famous lament in "Brise marine": "La chair est triste, hélas! Et j'ai lu tous les livres" (Life is sad, alas, and I have read all the books).

thieves. In an epistle, one of them warns his addressee against "the subterfuges of thieves, bandits, vagabonds, alchemists, merchants, artisans of all kinds, warmongers, parasites, and profiteers."

The first thought that comes to mind is that al-Jāhiz wrote his book "against misers." That is what is generally believed, and it seems only natural. Which reader would not spontaneously side with generosity? Which reader does not remember funny stories told at the expense of misers, plays in which they are ridiculed, and satires where miserliness is depicted as a despicable vice, a repugnant flaw? If then al-Jāhiz is writing about misers, it can only be against them. How could one suppose otherwise? Does he not recount many stories where they are ridiculed, mocked, and vilified? Does he not take malicious pleasure in exposing their distasteful calculations, their meanness, and their base behavior?

Were al-Jāhiz's work to be limited to this aspect of the question, it would be of only minor interest. It is certainly true that, from the prologue on, he challenges misers and presents his book as a satire on their behavior. As he notes, they are unable to understand "the ugliness of the term 'miser,' the shame surrounding this qualifier, and the harm that it causes those who deserve to be called by it." However, against all expectations, he adds that, in defending miserliness, they use "some pertinent arguments and elegant and beautifully concise sentences." The book opens under the sign of a fundamental ambiguity: the satirical treatment of misers is counterbalanced by praise for their eloquence. Repulsion is linked to admiration.

But who is speaking in the preface? The author, of course. However, when one reads it with due attention, one realizes that the author is not the only one talking. Many passages are attributed to the reader, and one sometimes has difficulty separating the voices and recognizing the source of the pronouncement. The following passage, for example, contains a contradictory judgment concerning misers: "You have asked me to explain to you what has troubled their minds and distorted their understanding and what has made them blind and unbalanced. [You have begged me to provide you with] the reason for their resistance to truth and their denial of evidence; [to analyze for you] this heterogeneous temperament, this contradictory character, one in which, alongside gross fatuousness, we can find a dazzling intelligence; [to show you] why the luminous whole remains hidden from them, while they grasp at obscure details."

The reader has a great appetite for knowledge, an appetite whetted by the preliminary knowledge that he has about the "heterogeneous temperament" of misers. Perhaps he knows more than he admits, concealing his knowledge behind a veil of modesty. What is certain is that, for him, miserliness is not something alien, a simple object of curiosity. Actually, he is wracked by doubt when it comes to miserliness, an uncertainty regarding his own situation: "You claim that you have a great need to know these questions and that a goodhearted man is never endowed with this particular topic. If, after protecting your goods from thieves, I shelter your honor in the face of critics, you tell me that I should have done much more for you than any affectionate father or tender mother." The honor (*'ird*) of the reader is at stake. Only the process of reading this work will allow the author to protect it, just as reading the *Tasnīf hiyal al-lusūs* has allowed him to protect the reader's property. In other words, the reader is not protected against stinginess; al-Jāhiz has bothered to write his book with the principal purpose of helping the reader confront and overcome it. The reader is perhaps a miser in denial or someone who can attain full self-knowledge only after deepening his awareness through a detailed study of avarice: "If, when you examine these defects, your attention is attracted by one of [your own] faults that has thus far escaped you, you will then appreciate its impact and will thereafter avoid it.[. . .] However, if concern for your goods is greater than your patient efforts [to spend], then you will hide and isolate yourself with your provisions, living peacefully like most common mortals." Here the reader is intimately linked to the topic of the book and invited to indulge in introspection, the goal being to detect thereby a hidden "fault," to eradicate it, or, if he is unable to do so, to tolerate it and take full responsibility for it. An axiom of life will have been derived from reading the book, and the reader will be grateful to al-Jāhiz for having allowed him to find himself, to probe his deepest tendencies, and to discover *his* truth.

But one may well ask where the problem lies? What is it that is tormenting the reader and causing all this discussion? Bit by bit we learn that it is at once the lure of generosity and the embarrassment at the costs involved. The reader is implicitly someone who is well-off;[2] he is in a position to assume some expenses, to offer meals (food is at the core of the book and, as we shall see, is inseparable from the question of avarice). But he is faced with a dilemma: withdrawal or advance, retreat or deployment, shade or light? Nobody is forcing him to be liberal toward others, to invite them so as to "gain their friendship by eating with them." If he chooses to act in this manner, the slightest trace of stinginess will expose him to the criticism of his tablemates; if he does not act in such a fashion, he will be condemned to living

2. Al-Jāhiz is scarcely interested in people who are destitute, deprived, in need, or vegetating in an obscure condition.

in denial, an unknown. As long as he has not made up his mind, he will remain perplexed and miserable: "If indecisive struggles arise between your own temperament and yourself, and if you fight with similar and equal weapons, you will then satisfy your self-respect by no longer being exposed [to blame] and your sense of economy by abandoning all affectation. You will then see that being exempt from all criticism already constitutes a gain, while a preference for level-headedness over delusion is a demonstration of firmness." In the last analysis, the reader has to make up his mind whether to eat alone or with guests.

To better grasp the implications of this dilemma, let us examine a story, or rather a scene, that amazed al-Jāhiz. It is found in the chapter on the people of Khurāsān, a people "renowned for their greed." Al-Jāhiz describes watching about fifty donkey drivers from Khurāsān having lunch: "Out of this fifty, there were no two of them eating together, even though they were sitting close to each another and chatting. This seems incredible!" Incredible to whom? For al-Jāhiz, of course, but also for the reader whom he is addressing. Otherwise, he would not have been satisfied with simply including an exclamation and would have proceeded to explain his astonishment. How can one eat alone? All the donkey drivers are from Khurāsān; they have the same trade, the same language, and the same points of reference; they are even "sitting close to each another," and yet they are irrevocably separated because they refuse to eat together. We have the feeling that, for al-Jāhiz, they have not completely risen above the level of animality: half-human, half-beast. They are stripped of any true community spirit. Although they do certainly talk to each other, they especially need to share their food communally in order to perfect their humanity. However, as far as the donkey drivers are concerned, the failure to share their meal is completely normal and needs no justification. They are not the least bit concerned about al-Jāhiz's gaze, and in any case he has not asked them to explain the reasons for their behavior. After all, they are donkey drivers, and we all are familiar with the contempt shown by well-read people in olden times toward those of lower status.

In what way is the act of eating alone reprehensible? How does it denote avarice (for everyone realizes that al-Jāhiz interprets the spectacle in this manner)? Does each donkey driver fear that food sharing will be to his detriment? Just prior to this scene, al-Jāhiz has narrated how some Khurāsānis have chipped in to buy oil for the lamp; "however, one of them refused to share the expense with his companions. Therefore, when the lamp was brought, they blindfolded him with a handkerchief." Another anecdote, whose hero this time is an educated man, contains an unexpected and disconcerting argument in favor of solitary meals: "Abū Nuwās told me that on the boat taking them to Baghdad there was an individual who was a member of the intellectual elite of Khurāsān. Since he was eating alone, I asked him why. 'It is not me you should ask,' he replied, 'but rather those who are eating together. That is not natural. I consider that, by eating alone, I'm following the norm. Were I to take my meals with other people, I would be departing from it.'" So Abū Nuwās did not understand why this learned Khurāsāni was eating alone, and, for his part, the latter could not understand why his interlocutor needed to eat with a group. Two surprises, then, with contrasting paths, two opposing norms. The Khurāsāni first points out that the question he has been asked is not pertinent, then goes on to explain that his behavior is perfectly in keeping with nature, whereas Abū Nuwās's is a sinful innovation, a perversion. Why would he forsake nature in order to adopt a convention for which he can see no reason? It is noteworthy that Abū Nuwās does not respond to this defender of nature with a discourse on *culture*. Is he taken by surprise, or does he instead depend on the complicity of the addressee to deduce the implicit rule that the Khurāsāni is infringing? In any case, for him as for al-Jāhiz, eating meals with other people signifies association, solidarity, altruism and marks a high degree of humanity.[3]

The chapter in the book that is devoted to al-Hārithī may allow us to understand better the reader's dilemma: "Someone recently said to al-Hārithī: 'By God, you prepare excellent and hearty meals, you shoulder lots of expenses, and you pay plenty to the baker, the chef, the roaster[. . .]. And yet, despite all these expenses, you invoke as witness to your affluence neither an enemy in order to embarrass him nor a friend to delight him nor an ignoramus to notify him [of your generosity] nor a visitor to honor him nor a grateful person to sustain [his gratitude].'" By eating alone, al-Hārithī is forgoing a certain prestige in the eyes of both friends and enemies. Invitations to guests earn one esteem and renown. Guests will regale you with expressions of appreciation and admiration. The offer of a meal also entails eulogies whose benefit is assured. However, al-Hārithī remains deaf to this reasoning. In order to justify his behavior, he invokes bad manners witnessed at the guest table. In a lengthy harangue (instead of offering a meal, he serves up a speech), he details the bad table manners that turn a group meal, one that is supposed in principle to be a manifestation of civility, into a disgusting display of bestiality. Here is an example of an

3. Al-Jāhiz returns to this question at the end of the epistle of Abū al-'As: "One criticizes people who eat alone and one adds: 'Ibn 'Umar has never eaten alone; Hassan [al-Basrī] has never eaten alone.'"

unpleasant guest: "When he ate, he lost his wits. Eyes bulging, he was nothing but a drunkard, all worked up and out of breath. His expression turned gloomy, and his mouth dried up. He neither heard nor saw anything.[. . .] On the other hand, every time I've seen him, he's looked like someone craving vengeance, a vindictive, jealous person." It has been suggested that this speech is intended to conceal the person's [the unpleasant guest's] avarice, which is not totally wrong. However, let us not forget that he assumes "huge expenses" and does not impose any deprivations on himself. Besides, what he says is reported without any comment on al-Jāhiz's part; in the chapter in which he appears, he is never described as being miserly (even if he is elsewhere classified as a miser). He has made a choice and freed himself from the indecision that torments the "reader."

The Book of Misers is a huge banquet where people from all walks of life rub elbows: spendthrifts, misers, governors, parasites, gluttons, philologists, and theologians. The most varied dishes are served there. Let us reiterate that most of the scenes in the book concern cooking, nutrition, and intimate or ceremonial meals.[4] The very diversity of dishes presented to guests is proportionate to the variety of subjects treated by al-Jāhiz. Everything has been arranged in order to satisfy the reader's appetite: "In this book you will find three things: original arguments, subtle ruses, and amusing anecdotes. You will soon discover that, if the serious matters aggravate you, there is no shortage of things to make you laugh and amuse you." Invited to a feast where all kind of dishes are offered, the reader will not be bored. Good

4. Thus, the last chapter, which deals with the diet of ancient Arabs, no longer appears to be a digression.

humor is always at hand, the amusing being blended with the serious.

Having drawn attention to the work's variegated features in the preface, al-Jāhiz then launches into a long disquisition in which he both lauds and denigrates tears, then laughter. The pretext is that the book combines the comic and serious; on this topic we can cite many a passage in al-Jāhiz's book in which the fear of boring the reader is evident. The diversity of subject matter, the various points of view, digressions, interpellations to the reader, attempts to relate to, provoke, and involve the reader are all just so many devices aimed at staving off boredom, that well-known enemy of reading.[5] But the great characteristic of al-Jāhiz remains, as his contemporary Ibn Qutaybah duly noted in taking him to task for it, his propensity to "do something and then its opposite." An example is the praise and condemnation of tears as well as laughter.[6] In tackling *The Book of Misers*, we should keep this characteristic in mind in that praise of and satire toward miserliness are mixed in an inextricable way.

Again in the preface, al-Jāhiz refers to another of his works, *Kitāb al masā'il* (The book of questions), where among the topics he examines are arguments proposed by other authors "to eliminate jealousy," "to elevate the lie to the

5. With many ancient authors, "narration of some spicy anecdotes that cause laughter" is expressed through a metaphor relative to diet: the *ihmād*, which consists of giving camels bitter salsuginosus plants of a *hamd* type (see Biberstein Kazimirski 1860). Al-Jāhiz makes such an allusion in *Misers* when he mentions Abū Nuwās, who "was eating at the table of Ismā'īl ibn Nawbakht the same way the camels graze on some *hamd* after having for a long time eaten the *khulla*."

6. See also the chapter on Tammām ibn Ja'far, a disconcerting sophist.

rank of sincerity and to lower the latter to that of a lie," and to pretend that "forgetfulness is preferable to a too reliable memory." This is a case in which propositions are placed in confrontation with commonly accepted opinions. We do not know why al-Jāhiz mentions them; it seems too easy simply to blame his tendency to digress. However, when we read the preface carefully, we notice that such paradoxical reasoning is mentioned in a context in which he claims that misers support "what everybody else agrees to disapprove of" and take pride in "a defect unanimously stigmatized." We can then see a link between the paradoxes revealed in *The Book of Questions* and the paradox inherent in *The Book of Misers*: an unusual view of things, of human relationships, of the world.

If the preface is ambiguous, with two voices—the discourse being shared by the author and the reader—what about the rest of the book? In it we find anecdotes, generally short, "chosen from among those of our friends and those that we have witnessed." We also find some rather lengthy speeches given by misers. Most of al-Jāhiz's direct discourse is quite limited; he habitually turns the floor over to the misers, *placing the words in their mouths*, just as he does with the reader. Being neither greedy nor selfish like some of the eaters he describes, he does not monopolize the speech or reserve it primarily for himself alone. Yet again the book is a banquet where food and speech are destined to be fairly shared among the various guests.[7]

Al-Jāhiz's generosity manifests itself in an even more subtle manner. The speech that he *turns over* to misers is actually attributed to them, even though in all probability he himself is the creator of the speeches that he *attributes* to

7. On the literature of banquets, see Jeanneret 1991.

them. This means that he identifies with them, that he speaks their language, and that, at least temporarily, he adopts their way of seeing things. Furthermore, some of his readers have suspected him of being a miser himself, maintaining that since he has depicted avarice so well, it is no doubt because he was, himself, a skinflint. We thus arrive at this delicious scenario: al-Jāhiz suspects his reader is a miser, while the latter suspects that al-Jāhiz is one himself.

However, it is not that simple. As we know, al-Jāhiz follows suit by turning the floor over to advocates of generosity and various speakers who lash out at avarice. A long debate takes place in which two irreconcilable points of view are at loggerheads from the beginning to the end of the book. In general, misers do not make the first move. They are in a defensive posture, and their speech constitutes a reaction to blame, to provocation. Now, when we examine the book's composition, we notice that the misers' speech is richer and more elaborate than that of their adversaries. It involves both oral speech (refutations, reprimands, harangues, and recommendations by Thawrī, by Ibn al-Mu'ammal, by Khālid ibn Yazīd, and so on[8]) and the written word (three epistles written by notorious misers—Sahl ibn Hārūn, al-Kindī, and Ibn al-Thaw'am—as opposed to a single epistle composed by a partisan of generosity, Abū al-'As). Obviously, this creates an imbalance in favor of avarice.

The Jāhizian miser is not parsimonious with his words; he dispenses them generously, freely providing lessons on economy and teaching the principles of efficient management of one's goods. His companionship is sought "because

8. Ibn Yazīd is very special: reading the speech that he delivers on his deathbed with an extraordinary energy, how can we not think of Faust?

of the originality of his behavior and comments." The truth is that each miser is distinguished by a particular trait that may turn out to be complex. Ahmad al-Khārakī, for example, "was miserly and vain, which is the most irritating." Abū Sa'īd al-Madā'inī "was not only a miser, but also excessively proud and sensitive to slurs." One day, in a fit of anger and in defense of his dignity, this usurer tore up an acknowledgment of a debt of a thousand dinars. Abrupt shifts and about-faces of this kind are far from rare. The appeal of avarice is sometimes outshone by that of generosity, even waste. One miser may tear his tunic after drinking wine or listening to music, whereas another may not hesitate to "organize a genuine feast every day." A third "may be a miser with food but give generously of his money." A fourth may "succumb to a passion for female singers and eunuchs." We find ourselves faced with the paradoxical situation in which misers invite people to a reception, whereas their guests, even as they are blaming their host's miserliness, "want to be invited but not have to invite anyone themselves." A topsy-turvy world: misers who are generous and even lavish, others who are niggardly and greedy but still advocates of generosity. Avarice is detected in the people who condemn it, whereas it is possible to detect generosity in the behavior of those people among whom one would never expect to find it.

If, on the whole, the discourse of argumentation redounds to the misers' benefit, what about the anecdotes? For the most part, they are taken over by narrators who are (or believe themselves to be) generous. The anecdotes are told to a sympathetic audience that has already been won over to their cause. There is a genuine pleasure in narrating and listening to stories about misers, stories destined to provoke laughter and implicitly to instill the concept of generosity in the listener's mind.

However, al-Jāhiz's work also contains anecdotes about misers narrated by misers to misers this time. Abū Sa'īd al-Madā'inī "organized gatherings in which usurers and misers took part, discussing economic principles." The *masjidī* "would get together in the Great Mosque.[. . .] During their meetings in select groups, the conversation would revolve around the chapter [on economy] that they had discussed and studied as a group. The aim was to absorb some advantageous lessons and get a little pleasure in talking about the topic." A source of pleasure, the story also teaches them through example and may also involve "reducing their expenses and turning their fortune to good account." It also provides them with information about the antics and exploits of misers who, having surpassed others in the macerations and mortifications that they have endured and the penance they have imposed on themselves, have attained the rank of champions, even "saints," insofar as some of the strategies and maneuvers they have employed "are not obtained by reasoning" but "come from divine assistance and favor!" Exemplary figures from the past are invoked alongside contemporary models, among them the caliph 'Umar and the noted ascetic Hassan al-Basrī. Miserliness is thus lived as a rite of initiation, a fierce and heroic battle waged against the treacherous soul that leads one into temptation. This is what al-Kindī declares, and his sentiments are recorded by a disciple with both veneration and admiration: "The soul is in fact attracted by the new and unexpected. Novelty may appear gentle and pleasant, charming and seductive. However, when we challenge its nature, it surrenders because the soul is fickle: it is at once ferocious and familiar. As long as we burden it, it will bear up, but if we neglect it, it deteriorates."

As much as the miser may love stories about "savings," he is equally distrustful of stories that advocate "prodigality" and celebrate the merits of generous people: "Do not come to me with stories told by parasites or with the spells cast by deceptive folk.[. . .] Do not come to relate to me those fantastic stories that exist only in overblown poems, fabricated stories, and apocryphal books." The distrust that misers feel toward this type of story is equaled only by their scorn for poetry, starting with pre-Islamic poetry that exalts excessive and ostentatious spending—to wit, the potlatch. The ideal that this poetry urges one to admire is that of the sayyid, the chief who not only shows courage in combat but also feeds his clan well and gives himself over to practices that entail the destruction of goods as lavish offerings, games of chance, and drinking scenes (see Hamori 1974, 11). It is precisely against this custom of the Jāhiliyya period, "the era of ignorance," that misers are struggling.

In some ways, al-Jāhiz's book is written to counter the system of gift giving, the values conveyed by pre-Islamic poetry (see Mauss 1979). In such a context, the potlatch appears to show a kind of behavior that, if not actually senseless, is at least anachronistic; possibly justifiable in an archaic collectivity such as a tribal organization, it seems misplaced in large urban centers such as Basra, where individuals from various social origins and cultures are thrust together and where any unanimity of values is fractured. Times have changed, and so has the space. In *The Book of Misers*, the great desert as described in early poetry has given way to an urban landscape with interior scenes (palaces, houses, and mosques) and exterior scenes marked by "the collision of beast of burden, crowds, and jostling masses" (streets, shops, markets, rivers, and boats). Ethnic origins certainly are not forgotten, and yet they no longer play a decisive role. In the new metropolitan and multiracial context in which the influence of writing continues to grow, the individual knows that his clan and genealogy will not be of great assistance to him and, above all, that he has to depend on his own merit (Benabdelali 1999). If Jāhizian misers are pessimists, if they "accumulate many frightening subjects and lessen their share of hope," as their adversaries enjoy reminding them, it is because they are convinced that one can expect nothing from others;[9] wealth is the only distinction in which they can take pride.

In spite of the changes that have occurred in social life, the potlatch culture has managed to survive in the form of proverbs, sayings, and poetry in particular. The poets—people "who would wish to see all men exceed the bounds of prodigality, reaching to the extent of sheer folly, profiteers living at the expense of others"—are the inveterate enemies of misers. The latter respond to their attackers by calling them beggars and moochers: "Beware of their spells and the traps they set for you. Protect your fortune against all the tricks they are plotting and do not forget that their sorcery can lull the mind into sleep and dazzle the eyes." Moreover, Jāhizian misers do not compose verses; they are dedicated to writing prose. The bad-mouthing of generosity thus goes hand in hand with the discrediting of poetry, whereas the promotion of avarice is implicitly accompanied by a valorization of prose. If poetry that flatters and troubles the mind is synonymous with lies, then prose is the site of truth. Which prose? That of reasoning and argumentation: misers are dialecticians, and the genre they favor is the *risāla* (epistle), a genre that may have been cultivated in the past but in the new

9. One of their adversaries goes so far as to accuse them perfidiously of having "less confidence in God" than generous people: "Taking as a pretext the vicissitudes of fate and mistrust that we should have as compared with the reversal of fate, the miser simply hides his defiance toward Him who creates these reversals."

context is no longer seen as the preserve of official circles, having more and more supplanted poetry.

The promotion of reason and writing is also a promotion of economy. In al-Jāhiz's work, there is, as we might expect, a disputation over the label *avarice*, a difference of opinion as to the pertinence of this designation. What some people term avarice is for others "economy" (*iqtisād*) or "correction" (*islāh*). The misers present themselves as people who are setting things right. As *muslihūn*, reformers, they are, at least through a slight phonetic and semantic shift, akin to *sālihūn*, people who are upright, honest, pious, and virtuous.

10 To Lie Once a Year

In *A Thousand and One Nights*, there is often a misfortune, a loss, or a want that impels the narration. One character tells how he became one-eyed, another how the lower half of his body was petrified, and still another how his face became as yellow as saffron. In "The Tale of Ayyub the Shopkeeper, His Son Ghānim,. and His Daughter Fitna," three black slaves relate how they became eunuchs (and it should be mentioned in passing that, in their confessions, these eunuchs are by their own admission fond of human flesh, raising the interesting question as to whether there is some relationship between cannibalism and eunuchry). The first slave is castrated for having deflowered his master's daughter, the second for lying, and the third for fornicating with his mistress and her son. It is the story of the second of these slaves, whose name is Kāfūr (Camphor) that concerns us here (see Galland 1965, 1:187–92).

Ever since his earliest childhood, Kāfūr had developed the habit of inventing one lie every year. He was eight years old when a merchant bought him in spite of this vice. At first, all went well: "With the beginning of the new year, everything looked promising: it was a blessed year, when everything grew profusely." So his master invited his friends to a park outside the city. At noon he sent the slave to bring "something" from the house, but instead of doing so Kāfūr told his mistress that an old wall had collapsed on his master and his guests. "Upon hearing this news, the wife and children of my master screamed and tore their clothing and struck their faces. The neighbors came running. My mistress knocked over all the furniture [. . .] alongside her I lay waste to the shelves, destroying everything that was on them." Then he goes out ahead of the entire population of the city that is now heading to the place where his master is supposed to have died beneath the rubble. Arriving before them, he tells his master that the wall of the main room of the house has collapsed and his mistress and children are dead.

When the truth is finally discovered, Kāfūr is not impressed by his master's threats. "By God[. . .]," he tells him, "there's nothing you can do to me! You bought me knowing my vice. You'll have all the witnesses against you. They will testify that you accepted me this way, fully aware of the facts, and overlooking my defects: I lie, yes, I do, I fabricate one lie every year. However, this is only half a lie; I shall finish it by the end of the year. Then, it'll be complete."

Thus, once a year Kāfūr is consumed by a kind of fit, one that he cannot control. The temptation to lie is too strong for him; the only thing he can do is to create a story out of whole cloth.[1] So he behaves as though what he says were

1. His story is inserted in another one where it is also a question of lying. Zubayda, the wife of Harūn al-Rashīd, jealous of Qut al-Qulūb, the favorite concubine of the latter, drugs her and orders the three black eunuchs to bury her alive. Afterward, she asks a carpenter to make a wooden dummy, dresses it in Qut al-Qulūb's clothes, puts it in a shroud, and gives it a wonderful funeral. When the caliph learns about the death of his favorite concubine, he orders the body exhumed but does not dare pull back the shroud that conceals the pretence. In J. C. Mardrus's translation, the caliph "saw the wooden form covered with the shroud and thought that was his favorite concubine" (1980, 1:282). However, the

perfectly true. He does not seem to be aware of his lies, nor is he playing a role or pretending. One can therefore say that even as he lies, he is paradoxically being *sincere*. After the fit is over, he becomes normal—or, in other words, truthful.

His lie causes unrest and disorder. The entire city is in an uproar, and he is the one who causes a scandal. His tendency to lie seems to reveal in him a desire for revenge, to see his masters die and their property disappear. However, whatever his deeper motivations may be, he is adamant that one acknowledge that he has never hidden his fault (he has a squabbling, quibbling mind). From his point of view, he is acting honestly, so he feels no guilt and consequently no need for repentance. Lying does not arouse in him any problem of a moral nature, but rather one that is aesthetic in that, for him, lying is a kind of artifact and requires a year to be "completed" (the pre-Islamic poet Zuhayr ibn Abī Sulmā, considered one of "the slaves of poetry," takes one year to complete a poem). To his master, who wants to get rid of him, to be free of him, Kāfūr responds: "By God, you may well emancipate me, but, speaking for myself, I cannot write you off as long as the year has not ended and I have not completed my lie."

It is at "the beginning of the new year" that the scene takes place, which seems to coincide in the text with spring and nature's renewal. Just as the earth produces buds and fruits, so does Kāfūr produce lies. Nature's fertility and vegetal profusion correspond to the fecundity of his imagination.

---

latter will be saved by Ghanim, who has fallen in love with her. As soon as she has told him her story, he realizes that he would certainly lose his life if the caliph were to learn the truth. While waiting, he does not dare make any further amorous advances to her; he is virtually castrated. Whereas Kāfūr is actually castrated for talking, Ghanim is castrated for listening. We do not tell a story or listen to one with impunity.

One wonders if this story does not contain a vestige of the custom of lying once a year at the beginning of April (the old Roman calendar began with this month). It seems that for the Romans this Indo-European custom of celebrating the New Year was related to Fools' Day (Quirinalia) and to the carnival. In this tale from *A Thousand and One Nights*, one can perceive a more or less distinct echo of [this custom] in the form of the procession that heads to the place where the master and his friends are supposedly buried. This may perhaps explain the right to lie with impunity as claimed by Kāfūr.

However, the master does not see it that way. He has him castrated, thus cutting off his procreative organ (when he is at most nine years old). "Just as you have broken my heart with regard to what I loved the most," he tells the slave, "so have I done the same thing to you." Indeed. Unlike the two other slaves to whom he tells his story, Kāfūr has not committed a sin of the flesh, but rather one of the tongue. If there is an organ he cares for and for which he has an irrepressible need, it is indeed his tongue. The vengeance of the master is thus incomplete, just as Kāfūr's lie is incomplete.

In my book *L'Œil et l'aiguille* (The eye and the needle, 1992), I was led to wonder if Kāfūr had given up his annual lie after he was castrated. It occurred to me that after receiving such a punishment, he would change—all the more because he himself announced that his powers had diminished with the loss of his "eggs." However, the text specifies that this was not the case: "But everywhere they sold me after that, I kept on causing one disaster after another." These later lies, however, are not recounted. Obviously, one can also wonder if he may have been lying when he said he had lied and if indeed the very story that he was telling the two eunuchs was not in fact governed by his annual propensity for lying.

11 Is *A Thousand and One Nights* a Boring Book?

*I*n the eyes of well-read Arabs in the premodern era, the book *A Thousand and One Nights* is just about right for simple minds. In fact, I myself read it when I was a child; there's nothing new about that because, for many readers, it is linked to childhood, just as *Le Chat Botté* (Puss-in-Boots) and *Peau d'Ane* (Donkey Skin)[1] are. Occasionally I have claimed that it was the first book I ever read, but now I am no longer so sure. Behind such a claim there obviously lies a desire on my part to benefit somehow from the prestige of this work of art. What can be more worthwhile than starting one's reading career with *A Thousand and One Nights*? However the perception of what constitutes the first book to be read is by no means simple, often being based on a deliberate reconstruction of the past. Even so, let us assume, because it suits my purpose to do so, that the *Nights* is in fact the first book that I read.

What can I now make of still another claim—namely, that I liked it. Really? A formidable question indeed, for who on earth would dare state the opposite today? Who would

1. *Translators' note*: Both tales by Charles Perrault.

one take me for if I were to declare that I found it merely mediocre? In fact, I cannot truly affirm anything; I cannot even say that I read it. I certainly held it in my hands (the Beirut edition, duly expurgated, yet nicely presented), but I haven't the slightest recollection of any sense of amazement at this or that story. Perhaps I was not even able to read at that time. After all, reading stories demands not only a knowledge of the language, but also the acquisition of a certain number of narrative codes. However, at about the same time I had been reading *Sirat 'Antara* (The romance of 'Antara), and I am sure that I was profoundly moved by that. I had only the two first volumes of this epic novel, and I spent months, indeed years, feverishly searching for the remaining volumes because I knew the story was very long—all in vain.

Now, thirty years later, I have reread (or perhaps I should say "read") the *Nights*, but curiously enough I have not reread *'Antara* (and probably never will). So why has the *Nights* been thus privileged? What has prompted me to revisit it? It is better to say it straight out: not nostalgia, that's for sure. Another reason was involved, one of which I was not really aware. Reading or rereading a text is not always the result of a personal decision; the decision often originates with one mediating factor or another. Would I have taken up the *Nights* again if I had not read Voltaire's *Zadig* (Zadig, or The book of fate), Diderot's *Jacques le fataliste* (Jacques the fatalist and his master), and Crébillon's novel *Le Sopha* (The sofa: A moral tale), as well as Proust's *A la recherche du temps perdu* (*Remembrance of Things Past*). After all, Proust frequently refers to it and uses it as one of his two models of writing, the other being Saint-Simon. Nor is that all: in the 1960s, there was the sudden blossoming of structural analyses of narrative, a trend that made a fuss over *A Thousand and One Nights*. Whence my sense of duty to return to it.

Nevertheless, I am unable to rid myself of the feeling that my work is insignificant. I would certainly not have felt the same way if I had cast my lot with another work—that of Tawhīdī or Mutanabbī, for example. In such a case, my point of departure would have been one of tangible acumen, of knowledge accumulated through successive generations. In the case of the *Nights*, however, the Arabic tradition remains virtually silent. By becoming interested in the *Nights* again, I joined a European tradition, one that started with [Antoine] Galland [1646–1715]. In other words, I was placing myself outside the context of the Arabic literary tradition. Besides, is *A Thousand and One Nights* part of that literary tradition? It seems to me that that tradition can get along without the *Nights*; in fact, it has gotten along very well without it so far. The Arabic literary tradition would still be the same if the *Nights* had never existed, whereas its landscape would obviously look completely different without the *Mu'allaqāt* (The suspended poems), for example, those famous "suspended" odes, or without the *maqāmāt* (assemblies). In more or less recent accounts of Arabic literature, the *Nights* does not appear listed under any of the commonly encountered headings. It is not associated with any chronology, for example, even though we are aware that one of the first versions of the collection is contemporaneous with al-Hamadhānī (d. 1008) and al-Tanūkhī (d. 994), nor do they appear in chapters dedicated to prose, to be placed alongside *Kalila and Dimna* or *Risālat-al-ghufrān* (Epistle of forgiveness). They are cited only at the end of the day, a gesture to set one's mind at rest, in the vicinity of the *Romances of Dhat al-Himma* (Tale of Lady Delhemma) and *Sayf ibn Dhī Yazan* (Tale of Sayf ibn Dhi Yazan), alongside other works of indeterminate status.

It goes without saying that the *Nights* are not part of the canon of classical works in Arabic. As far as I am concerned, the principles behind the creation of this canon remain a mystery. I cannot determine how it is that some texts, whether in verse or prose, have managed to impose themselves, at the conclusion of a varyingly lengthy process, so as to become unavoidable points of reference. To me it seems appropriate to call them "classics," an ascribing of quality that I can find no equivalent for in Arabic, but that has the advantage of focusing attention on *class*. I am not using the term here in order to define the production of a given period, for any text adopted by the learned class is "classic," integrated as it is into a corpus of texts and destined to be taught in class.

To attain this status, the text must possess a certain number of properties. In the first place, it is linked to the name of an author. In Arabic culture, a text without an author is considered to be an aberration; in fact, there are very few anonymous texts. The origin of this prerequisite lies, no doubt, in the critical methods that have accompanied the compilation of the Prophet's sayings (hadith). Just as there are works devoted to the transmitters of these sayings, there are others concerning literary figures, biographies that collect the maximum amount of information related to them—their date of birth and (especially) the date of their death, details about their careers, anecdotes that focus on their image, extracts from their works, judgments by their contemporaries, and reflections on the controversies they may have provoked. Here we should note that any text about which we know only the author's name and nothing else suffers from this reality regardless of its quality. Such is the case, for example, with Abu-l-Mutahhar al-Azdi's *Hikāyat Abī-l-Qāsim* (The story of Abu al-Qasim), a text that would have known a better fate if it were proved to have been written, as some suggest, by al-Tawhīdī.

A stress on authorship has a bearing on another feature: the classic text is necessarily tied to the act of writing, even if at the earliest stages in the tradition it may have been transmitted only orally. Such texts have to be presented in a fixed form, although this ideal has not always been achieved. Thus, al-Hamadhānī's manuscripts contain variants, probably because the author, who died prematurely, did not have the time to put the finishing touches on his work and present it in final form. The same does not apply to al-Harīrī's *Maqāmāt*, for example, and on that topic it is useful to recall a very significant anecdote: when a reader suggested a way in which al-Harīrī might improve an expression, he admitted the aptness of the remark but went on to state that he would not adopt the suggestion because he had already checked the accuracy of seven hundred copies of his *maqāmāt* and given permission to transmit them (a practice known as *ijāza*).

The classical text is also characterized by a noble, imposing style, one that allows for trivial or dialectal expressions only when an anecdote is being recorded or a charming piece of discourse is being reproduced, whose effect may well be weakened if strict rules of lexicology and syntax are applied. Whenever such an assault on accepted style, motivated by "propriety" (or "congruence"), occurs, it is of necessity accompanied by a justification that is duly expressed. The phenomenon can be noted, for example, in the works of al-Jāhiz, Ibn Qutaybah, and Abu-l-Mutahhar al-Azdi (and we might note that in the case of the latter author the role of vulgarisms is especially significant).

Written in a language that is clearly distinguished from that of speech, the classic text is opaque, without immediate access, and consequently calls for commentary. It is not revealed fully until it is explained, translated into another discourse. Because such texts are destined to be taught, the authors themselves sometimes assume responsibility for this task—as is the case with, for example, al-Maʿarrī, al-Harīrī, and al-Zamakhsharī.

However, because the classic text is inseparable from its commentary, it does not lend itself well to translation; a version in a foreign language is beyond its horizons. Al-Jāhiz's *Kitāb al-hayawān* (Book of animals) affirms that poetry is restive in transmission: in a new language it loses its principal constituent, the *nazm* or metrical structure, and emerges as a web of banalities. It is only in the original language that the poem is identifiable as such to itself; it cannot be translated or, at least in principle, *should* not be. Al-Jāhiz does not explicitly express this interdiction, but it logically emerges from his comments. We can even go so far as to say that many texts in prose (*Risālat al-ghufrān*, for example, and al-Harīrī's *Maqāmāt*) are weakened and compromised in translation. One might object to such a statement by noting that everything depends on the quality of the translator. However, that is not the question. What I am trying to stress concerns the attitude of classic authors regarding the translation of their works: they were completely unaware of the possibility (whereas today it is the principal concern of Arab writers) (see Kilito 2008). Al-Mutanabbī would undoubtedly have become furious if someone had suggested in his presence that his poems be translated into Latin, Hebrew, or Persian.

It now becomes clear that *A Thousand and One Nights* does not fulfill any of the characteristics that I have just listed. It has no author; it is found in different versions; its style is vulgar (even though it does not systematically scorn rhymed prose); it includes commentary; and it is not the object of instruction. However, the factor that occasioned its ill fortune in the past is precisely what blesses it with good fortune today, in that it is the most translated Arab book.[2] One might even suggest that the *Nights* begs to be translated and not least because the collection itself stems in large part from Indian and Persian sources. Such is its transparency that it hardly loses any of its force when rendered into another language.

Residing beyond the pale of the literary, the *Nights* is presented, in short, as a book of leisure, of pure pleasure. It is worth noting that a well-read person was not supposed to spend his time studying serious books; it was recommended that he vary his readings (a habit called *ihmād*) and renew his energies by dedicating himself in moderation to frivolity, laughter, and indolent pleasure. However, the *Nights* was in all likelihood not included in the menu. Well-read people snubbed it and maintained an almost complete silence concerning it. Ibn al-Nadim is one of the few to mention the *Nights*. He read it, although we do not know in what form; what is clear is that the book he had in his hands was not exactly the same as the one available today. Here is what he said about it: "I have the chance to see this text in its complete form: to tell the truth, it is a very poor book that narrates coldly."[3] In other words, it is a boring book.

Should we accuse him of being a bad reader and be outraged by his attitude? In fact, he was not disparaging only the *Nights*, and his opinions undoubtedly echo those of his well-read contemporaries—opinions, indeed, that did not change later. There would thus have been a kind of collective

2. And first in classical Arabic. We know that in the Boulaq edition 'Abd al-Rahmān al-Sharqāwī had the preposterous idea of improving the style of the *Nights* by rewriting [the stories] in an elevated language.

3. Ibn al-Nadim's version is translated and cited by Andre Miquel (Bencheikh, Miquel, and Bremond 1991, 13–15).

blindness regarding the quality and richness of the *Nights*. So how can we go against the collective judgment of so many centuries? We cannot dismiss it with a mere swipe of the hand, even if we do not agree with it. What is worse is that traces of the verdict survive, giving rise to a horrible suspicion: What if the *Nights* actually is boring, and we are the ones who are victims of a pandemic blindness that compels us to overestimate the value of the *Nights*? Besides, why do we feel obliged to keep on ensuring that it be defended and glorified? Why do we act as if we were somehow required to correct a millennium-old injustice? The ancients scorned *A Thousand and One Nights* because it did not conform to the classical norm. But in the name of what precisely do we appreciate it, and at what point in time did the change in reader reception come about?

In the Arab world, it occurred relatively recently. The pioneers of the Nahda [Renaissance or Awakening] movement, writing in the second half of the nineteenth century and the beginning of the twentieth century, had not completely divested themselves of classical attitudes. To my knowledge, none of them laid claim to the *Nights*. On the other hand, they undoubtedly referred to the *maqāmāt* (al-Shīdyāq in *Al-Saq 'ala al-saq fi ma huwa al-Faryaq* [One leg crossed over the other] and al-Muwaylīhī in *Hadith 'Isa ibn Hisham* ['Isa Ibn Hisham's tale]. Thus, while the classical genre of the *maqāmāt* provided a requisite transition by contributing to the flowering of the Arabic novel, Shahrazād's tales were also available but remained an untapped source of any literary revival.

One can add at this point that since those early days Arab writers have largely compensated for this neglect. Interest in the *Nights* has not stopped growing; editions of it have multiplied, as have studies of it. In comparison, interest in the *maqāmāt* has lessened, if not more or less disappeared. The *maqāmah* discourse, based as it is on rhetorical exhibitionism, has ended up being considered a sterile and inhibiting legacy (indeed, they survived miraculously, thanks to the miniatures done by al-Wasitī in the thirteenth century, which have been reproduced on the cover of many publications on Arabic literature). We are thus witnessing a reversal: the *maqāmāt* have become unreadable, whereas the *Nights* is being read more and more. Thanks to Europeans, the Arabs came to realize one fine day that they possessed a treasure of whose value they had been totally unaware.

However, Ibn al-Nadim's judgment does not seem to have entirely disappeared. Otherwise why did we have to wait until 1984 for the appearance of a critical edition of the *Nights*? Critical attention of it was late in coming, and, in the eyes of many observers, its influence on Arabic literature has remained rather limited. Some poets allude to it, whereas certain prose writers (Taha Husayn, Tawfiq al-Hakīm, and Naguib Mahfūz, for example) find in it an example of the character of the tyrant.[4] However, in the works of these authors, it is rare to find the intimacy and complicitous familiarity with the *Nights* that we find in Proust or Borges. It must be said that the *Nights* has enjoyed a far greater influence in Europe than in the Arab world, and yet it is (or should be) one of the principal sources of pride for the Arabs. In the past, we have established parallels between Arabic culture and that of other peoples, in the process coming to the conclusion that poetry is the Arabs' greatest claim to glory. Today, as we

4. On the reception of the *Nights* in the Arab world today, see Ghazoul 1996, 34–149.

continue to practice the vain game that involves summarizing what Europeans owe to the Arabs, we are tempted to say that the principal merit of the Arabs is to have written the *Nights*. Would the Arabs have perceived themselves or been perceived in the same manner had this collection of tales not existed?

12 The New Dante

In his literary family tree, Juan Goytisolo reserves a significant space for Arabic literature. The titles of some of his works stress it: *Makbara*, *Crónicas sarracinas*, *En los reinos de taifa*, as well as *Barzakh*, which is of particular interest to us here.

Barzakh [originally] appeared in Spanish under the title *La Cuarantena* (*Quarantine* [Goytisolo 1994]). The number 40 plays an important role in the novel: the death of a female friend plunges the narrator-character into a period of mourning that, as required, lasts forty days. It is also the duration of "the aerial hell" over Baghdad (during the 1990–91 Gulf War). Furthermore, the narrator is in the process of writing a novel, *La Cuarentena* to be exact, which is composed of forty chapters. Because it is appropriate that he take a step back in relation to personal and international events, he finds the image of a sanitary cordon imposing itself on him: "Isn't the process of literary creation one of quarantine?" he wonders before adding that as soon as the reader becomes engrossed in a work, he "finds himself in quarantine as well, isolated from the world inside his bubble."

The title chosen for the French translation [*Barzakh*] is also a fortunate one: in the Islamic tradition, *barzakh* is the time period between a man's death and the day of his resurrection. The action of Goytisolo's novel takes place on two levels that are sometime difficult to distinguish. The narrator travels through real sites—Paris, Marrakesh, Cairo; he takes the plane, goes on automobile trips, bathes at the *hammām*, has tender conversations with his wife, and watches the news on television. But even as he loves his life, he also has dreams that run parallel to the concrete, tangible world, dreams in which another world opens out, ethereal, the *barzakh*, which is described by Ibn 'Arabī as follows: "When souls fly toward the intermediary world or *Barzakh*, they remain in possession of their bodies, adopting the subtle form that appears to us when we see ourselves in a dream."

The narrator moves with agility from one world to the other. In the afterlife, his female friend, a new Beatrice, serves as his guide (she always makes the gesture, both vain and touching, of picking up the Gauloises bleues cigarettes that he usually smokes). Dreams follow dreams, visions, hallucinations, where he sees himself dead, in the company of wandering souls. "Just as I was actually about to write the book, I died."

Where do these pictures come from? From books. The narrator is a reader who is influenced by his reading. What he lives becomes the reflection of what he reads, to such an extent that he is no longer of this world. So he repeats the experience of Don Quixote, although with the difference that this time it is not a matter of picaresque novels, but of texts that are mystical or pertain to life after death: Molinos's *Spiritual Guide*, *The Divine Comedy*, Ibn 'Arabī's works, and Bistāmī's sayings, as well as Hieronymus Bosch's paintings and Gustave Doré's prints. To this list we might add Kafka, that specialist in eschatological expectation. The narrator is summoned to appear before the court of auditors by Nakir and Munkar (the two angels, "expert accountants," "investigators," "examiners") and finds himself in an administration office where doors open and close, where he is made to wait, where no one pays any attention to him, and where finally he is not received by those who had originally summoned him. In another moment, the phone rings; Nakir and Munkar are announced to him, but there is no one at the other end of the line: "What was he to do? Hang up? Undermine the dignity and standing of the examiners at the risk of turning them against him? Were they not simply putting him to the test in order to gauge his patience and sense of respect for their authority?"

With this novel, Goytisolo deepens the views of Asin Palacio, the eminent scholar who in *La Escatalogia musulmana en la* Divina Comedia (Islamic eschatology in the *Divine Comedy*) has detailed Dante's debt to Arab culture and particularly to *Al-'Isrā' wal-Mi'rāj* (The book of Muhammad's ladder) (which recounts the Prophet Muhammad's journey to heaven), to the mystical visions of Ibn 'Arabī, and to the *Risālat al-ghufrān* (Epistle of forgiveness) by al-Ma'arrī. Goytisolo seems also to reconnect with an ancient tradition—namely, inquiries into the fate of the dead in the next world. In the atmosphere of competition between doctrines and divergent theological opinions, it is a question of knowing which profession of faith, which belief, secures salvation after death. Whence the importance of what one might term the heresiographical dream: the deceased appears to one of his acquaintances in a dream and reports what has happened to him (whether he has been rewarded or punished). The heresiographical dream often provides its author with the opportunity to settle a score with his adversaries and enemies.

Within the context of Arab culture, Goytisolo places special emphasis on the mystical dimension. Thus, he does not grant much importance to al-Ma'arrī, the blind poet, who is present in *Barzakh* only in this single line: "Gently tread upon the soil; it will soon be your grave."

However, is this really a verse by al-Ma'arrī? Or is the translation that has been used rather an approximation? In any case, the text from al-Ma'arrī is more powerful, more ironic: thinking about all the corpses resting within the ground, the poet says, "Let your step be gentle, for the earth's surface, I believe, consists of these corpses," a verse that is in perfect harmony with the state of souls in the *barzakh*, a world of nuances as described by Goytisolo after Ibn 'Arabī—the shades tread very softly upon the soil, they glide, delicate and nostalgic fledglings.

The Arab reader who reads *Barzakh* will feel that al-Ma'arrī has been neglected. It goes without saying that a novel has its own coherence, that it is *full* like an egg; there is nothing one can add to it or take from it without destroying its integrity. To tell Goytisolo that his novel lacks a character or a point of reference is to express an insanity. However, in the imagination of the reader steeped in the Arabic literary tradition, the afterlife is associated with al-Ma'arrī and his *Epistle of Forgiveness*, a work that describes with humor and in great detail the resurrection of the dead, judgment, and heaven and hell. As described by al-Ma'arrī, the afterlife is an immense banquet where poets rub shoulders with grammarians. His hero, Ibn al-Qārih, being a litterateur, can be resurrected only in the company of literary figures. But Goytisolo finds such a perspective most disagreeable:

> I can't picture you in one of those lively parties of which your compatriots are so fond, bringing together poets, novelists, critics, philologists, and grammarians, and you discussing literary subjects with them for eternity! What a cruel punishment it would be to be forced to tolerate

> the company of academics and courtiers, holders of medals, and recipients of a great deal of media attention, this whole cohort of asinine pen-pushers, Cavafy-esques poets, know-it-all muses, and other windbags inflated with their own conceited self-importance, the kind of people you have always avoided with horror!

Although al-Ma'arrī described the afterlife, he did not believe in resurrection. It is no doubt for that reason that Goytisolo does not come across him in *Barzakh*. However, perhaps they made an appointment somewhere else, in another novel.

13 Perec and al-Harīrī

The mention of al-Harīrī in Georges Perec's *La Vie mode d'emploi* (*Life: A User's Manual* [1987]) is rather surprising: this eleventh-century Arab writer from Basra is not well known in Europe. Beyond a few specialists, his name does not suggest anything to the French reader. That is also the case with dozens of other names from various cultures whose citation in *Life: A User's Manual* is apparently only meant to create what we might call an erudite impression. Yet the presence of al-Harīrī is not the result of pure chance.

In which context is he mentioned? On page 298 of *Life: A User's Manual*, Georges Perec reproduces the table of contents of an issue of the *Bulletin of the Linguistics Institute at Louvain*. Placed alongside Dr. Dinteville's doormat, this issue is part of a "pile of tied-up newspapers intended for students who periodically come to the building to collect old papers." We are left to wonder in passing what this linguistic bulletin might be doing on top of the other medical publications. Among the articles mentioned in the contents, there is one in English by L. Stefani, "Al-Harīrī Revisited. III. Crosswords and Isograms." We are obviously dealing here with the third installment of a larger study, the first two of which had already appeared in previous issues. L. Stefani, in "revisiting" al-Harīrī, dedicates this part of his study to the old Arab writer's verbal games. We will never know what other aspects of al-Harīrī had been studied in the earlier segments, but we can surmise that the first part invoked the circumstances involved in the composition of his magnum opus, the *Maqāmāt* (Assemblies), whereas the second part, after the *Maqāmāt* had been situated in the context of classical Arabic storytelling, analyzed its themes, notably the one that depicts the lowest social strata. In any case, L. Stefani presents his essay as a new attempt at understanding al-Harīrī. Nevertheless, to my knowledge this scholar does not appear among those interested in the author of the *Maqāmāt*. Perec mentions him again in the index but does not provide any information about him. It would seem that the author L. Stefani is pure fiction.

In the index, Perec does qualify al-Harīrī as an "Arab poet" and provides his birth and death dates (1054–1122). However, on this subject we must provide a further detail: al-Harīrī certainly wrote verse, but he is not really known as a poet. We should observe also that his work is not extensive. He wrote a didactic poem on grammar, *Mulhat al-i'rāb fī al-nahw*, as well as a book on lexicology, *Durrat al-ghawwās fī awhām al-khawass*. He is also the author of quite a few epistles, of which two are noteworthy owing to a particular structural characteristic: in one of them, every word contains the letter *s* and in the other a *sh*. However, if al-Harīrī is renowned, it is entirely thanks to his *Maqāmāt*, [a title using] a word that can be translated into French as *séances* and into English as something like *assemblies*. The *maqāmah* is a relatively short narrative written in a scholarly and obscure language: its hero is a well-read, eloquent beggar. We should also mention there that al-Harīrī is not the first to write such works: the founder of this narrative genre (that prefigures the picaresque novel in Spain) is al-Hamadhānī (d. 1008). However, al-Harīrī, the imitator, surpasses his model.

So how did Perec get to hear about al-Harīrī? When he was writing *Life: A User's Manual*, the *Maqāmāt* had long since been translated into English and German, but only a few of the "assemblies" had been translated into French, in some relatively inaccessible journals.[1] Whether Perec had read these or not, he was certainly familiar with the writing of al-Harīrī and particularly with his propensity for word games.[2] We may assume that he knew of al-Harīrī from this or that encyclopedia or manual on Arabic literature, but it is not out of the question that he may have known of him thanks to an article by Ernest Renan, "Les *Séances* de Hariri" (Hariri's *Assemblies*) (1859).

Curiously enough, the only time that Renan is mentioned in *Life: A User's Manual* is with regard to an ancestor of Dr. Dinteville, who "was thought to have discovered the secret of making diamonds from coal." Perec tells us that Renan "brings up his case in one of his chronicles (*Mélanges*, 47, *passim*)." Is there really such a chronicle by Renan? That would have to be checked. Such is often the case with Perec: we do not always know if his references are authentic. For example (still in connection with Dr. Dinteville), we learn that one of his ancestors was elevated to the nobility by Louis XIII and that Cadignan (a seventeenth-century French chronicler) "has left a striking portrait of this character, who seems to have been an unpleasant ruffian." However, this portrait is nothing but a clone of that of Panurge in *Pantagruel*! Reading Perec demands that we adopt a skeptical attitude similar

1. It was only in 1992 that René Khawam published an integral translation entitled *Le Livre des malins: Séances d'un vagabond de génie*.

2. "The grammarian and Arab poet Harīrī himself practiced the lipogram, but, it must be acknowledged, as an amateur" (Perec 1973, 84).

to what seems appropriate when we are reading Borges. So we are tempted to verify his references, but I have not done so for the chronicle attributed to Renan. In the meantime, a doubt, slight though it may be, still lingers. Even if the reference turns out to be real, the feeling that one has been conned would remain. The simple act of verification is the consequence of a hoax on Perec's part, a trap skillfully set into which I have fallen.

Perec does not mention Renan's article on al-Harīrī. However, Renan, for his part, knew Arabic and had read the *Maqāmāt*. Arab readers are well aware that one cannot tackle these texts without the help of a commentary, for they are full of archaisms and learned allusions; they are so obscure that with every line one has to refer to the explanations. We are undoubtedly dealing with a most difficult work; for that reason, it has been the subject of many analyses. It is perhaps the most explicated Arabic work after the Qur'ān. Obviously, when [it is] read in translation, the obscurity, at least on the lexical level, is alleviated and may even disappear, for the translation is actually an exegesis, a clarification. The most remarkable and curious comment is one made by Sylvestre de Sacy, who edited the *Maqāmāt* in 1822 and wrote a copious commentary on them—not in French, but in Arabic! Renan read al-Harīrī using this commentary.[3]

That is all well and good, one might say, but where is the connection with *Life: A User's Manual*? Let us emphasize that al-Harīrī is mentioned in the same breath as Dr. Dinteville, a character who has his own story, duly told in chapter XCVI of the novel. After defending a "thesis, dashed

3. His article that starts with Sylvestre de Sacy's praise is a review of the second edition published in 1853 by two of the latter's students.

off by some underpaid students" (in other words, he is not its author), he settled in Lavaur. Exploring in his attic one day, he "found a booklet in a trunk full of old family papers [. . .] entitled *De structura rerum*, whose author was one of his ancestors.[. . .] He decided to prepare a critical edition of this text." When the work was completed, he sent a copy to Professor LeBran-Chastel, but the latter sent it back, declaring it to be without interest and refusing, "for his part, to favor its publication in any way." Some years later Professor LeBran-Chastel published a series of works that amounted to nothing more than a copy of Dinteville's manuscript. Dinteville's thesis came from the pen of a student, and the publications of Professor LeBran-Chastel came from the pen of Dinteville!

In any case, Dinteville's work is comparable to that of Sylvestre de Sacy in that both of them prepared a critical edition of an old book: Dinteville *revisited* his ancestor, and Sylvestre de Sacy *revisited* al-Harīrī. In his turn, L. Stefani undertook a lengthy study of al-Harīrī: he published the third part, and nothing permits us to assume that it is the last one. The three cases involve a work of scholarship and an interest in old texts: medicine, as Rigaud de Dinteville, the ancestor, understood it, is antiquated and has been superseded, and al-Harīrī's style of writing is outmoded.

Ernest Renan provides the link that allows me to make this tentative, meandering, and admittedly speculative connection between al-Harīrī and Perec. Other parallels, no doubt more comfortable, might also be established.

Following the example of *Life: A User's Manual*, in which all continents and countries are represented or mentioned, the *Maqāmāt* also has a universal dimension: the title of each *maqāmah* invokes a land or city within "the Islamic empire." The heroes are tireless travelers, and ever since the book's publication it has circulated throughout all the lands where it has been introduced. As Renan himself points out, "Few works have exercised such a widespread literary influence as al-Harīrī's *Maqāmāt*. From the Volga to the Niger, from the Ganges to the Straits of Gibraltar, it has been the model of intelligence and beautiful style for all the peoples who have adopted Muhammad's language along with Islam."

However, al-Harīrī's contemporaries at first refused to recognize him as the true author of the *Maqāmāt*. Just as Professor LeBran-Chastel appropriated the work of Dr. Dinteville, it was thought that al-Harīrī had appropriated a manuscript he found in a traveling bag belonging to a Maghribi who had died under unknown circumstances (see chapter 1, pp. 13–14).

Another analogy: al-Harīrī's work is an amalgamation, for in it we find various genres, styles, registers, and tones as well as a literary appropriation of such nonliterary subjects as jurisprudence. Translated into several languages, it has been illustrated many times by painters, this being another form of translation or commentary. However, all things considered, it is an untranslatable book. One might say that in some respects al-Harīrī is an *oulipien*,[4] ahead of his time; he composed his work in accordance with a system of constraints. His *maqāmāt* are certainly autonomous, not narratively knitted together; even so, we can still find numerous

4. *Translators' note*: Ouvroir de Littérature Potentielle (whence OuLiPo, Oulipo, and *oulipien*), a loosely knit movement founded by Raymond Queneau and François Le Lionnais that was an offshoot of the "Pataphysique movement." Members of the group favored constraints of style and verbal necessity in writing and indulged in verbal games and tricks (puns, wrong division in phrases, palindromes, obscure historical and literary references, and so on).

thematic links between them. They are divided into five series of ten: the first of each series is "parenetic," the fifth and the tenth "comic," the sixth "literary." By "literary," we mean that the *maqāmah* is based on a verbal game—namely, the palindrome: some verses and epistles, read from beginning to end or from end to beginning, have the same alphabet sequence and consequently the same meaning.

The big question concerning verbal games, at least in some cases, is that they are not noticeable. Alliteration attracts attention ("le dur désir de durer" [the strong desire to last]), as does rhythmic or rhymed prose. But if I read this expression, "élu par cette crapule" (elected by this villain), a classic example of the palindrome in French, how am I supposed to know that this sentence can be read equally well from left to right or right to left while retaining the same meaning? Unless I happen to notice it by chance or through a sudden insight, I have no way of knowing. Al-Ḥarīrī encountered this dilemma and resolved it by telling us every time he carried out a trick. Perec himself is less explicit; he is not even the least so in *Life: A User's Manual.* And yet there are innumerable games in the novel, traps and constraints that the reader may pass by without even noticing them. Should we point them out or not? Perec cannot resist the temptation to invoke some of them in interviews and also, we might assume, in private remarks to friends. This is how we find out that the name "Calvino" [the Italian novelist] is hidden in the phrase "Le basset Optimus Maximus arrive à la nage à Calvi notant avec satisfaction que le maire l'attend avec un os" [The basset hound Optimus Maximus comes swimming to Calvi, noting with satisfaction that the mayor is waiting for him, holding a bone], whereas in another phrase, "Septime Sévère apprend que les négociations avec le Bey n'aboutiront que s'il lui donne sa soeur Septimia Octavilla" [Septimus Severus learns that the negotiations with the Bey will never reach an end unless he gives him his sister Septimia Octavilla], we find the name "Bénabou."[5]

Life: A User's Manual is favorite fare for two kinds of reader: first, those people who read it for its fine stories, its fine "novels"; second, those (the best?) who are aware of Perec's verbal games and who, not relying on the superficial appearance of the text, discover the word games and clever tricks that are involved. But who can boast of knowing all the constraints observed by Perec? Although we have discovered a great number of them, we suspect that many others also exist, irreparably hidden, but we must nevertheless endeavor to detect them. Whence the temptation to bring to the text a mystic, cabalistic, infinite reading.

There is a real pleasure in discovering that one text hides another, that an unforeseen reading is possible, even necessary. However, I must confess that I experienced considerable disappointment with the examples just mentioned. After a brief moment of enthusiasm, the thrill subsided: Is that all there is? No matter how vehemently I maintain that Perec is exploring the possibilities of language,[6] a bitter memory keeps coming back to spoil everything. Which memory is that? That of the "decadence" (real or imagined) of classical Arabic literature from the eleventh century on—or, to be more precise, since al-Harīrī. Rightly or wrongly, Arabs today ascribe the responsibility for "decadence" to this particular author and his disciples: their word games and verbal

5. *Translators' note*: We have been able to translate the first of these phrases in a way that conveys Perec's verbal play on Calvino's name, but one must examine the original French of the second phrase to locate in it the last name of Marcel Bénabou, one of the *oulipiens*. Did you find it?

6. See the fine study by Tzvetan Todorov (1999).

acrobatics are viewed as the principal cause of the calamity that ravaged belles-lettres for centuries. So when we learn of certain aspects of the *oulipien* program, we are obliged to give an indulgent smile. Perec is no al-Harīrī, that's for sure, and yet a disturbing sense of strangeness overcomes the Arab reader when, for example, he sets eyes on *La disparition* (A void).[7] That novel will in all likelihood never be translated into Arabic, or at least not any time soon.

7. *Translators' note*: *La disparition* is Perec's novel entirely composed of words that do not contain the letter "e."

14 Twenty-Four Hours in the Life of Averroës

While ruling Andalusia, King ʿAbd ar-Rahmān, alias "the Fugitive," harbored deep in his heart a nostalgia for Syria, his native land. One day, spotting a palm tree, he exclaimed: "You are, you too, O palm tree! / On foreign land" (from "Averroës's Search" in Borges 1993).

In "Averroës's Search," [Jorge Luis] Borges recalls this story and has the Córdoban philosopher say: "Singular privilege of poetry: words written by a king who missed the Orient served me, exiled in Africa, to express my nostalgia for Spain."

In his own way, Averroës was a nostalgic man. Born in Europe, he spent his entire life marked by Arabic desert poetry and indifferent to all other literature. The most dazzling illustration of this propensity is his commentary on the *Poetics* of Aristotle: he never realized that the work dealt mainly with theater. The thing that misled him is the Arabic translation on which he relied (probably the one by Mattā ibn Yūnus), in which the word *tragedy* is translated as "panegyric" and the word *comedy* as "satire": a grave misunderstanding that, as some would have it, prevented a connection with Greek literature. It is this misunderstanding that Borges describes in his own way in "Averroës's Search."

The tale opens with the philosopher in his library; he is writing his book criticizing the theologian al-Ghazālī (d. 1111), *Tahāfut al-tahāfut* (The incoherence of the incoherence):

> The pen sped along the page; arguments intertwined, irrefutable; but a slight preoccupation compromised Averroës's bliss.[. . .] The night before, two dubious words had stopped him at the threshold of the *Poetics*. Those words were *tragoedia* and *comoedia*. Years earlier he had already seen them in the third book of the *Rhetoric*; no one in Islam could make out what they meant. In vain he had exhausted Alexander of Aphrodisias's epistles; again in vain he had consulted the versions of the Nestorian Hunayn ibn Ishāq and Abu Bashar Meta. The two secret words are found in abundance in the text of the *Poetics*; it is impossible to escape them.

Thus it is that Averroës encounters two incomprehensible words at the threshold of the *Poetics*. We know that he knew neither Greek nor Syriac. Now, it was into Syriac that the *Poetics* was first translated; then an Arabic version was completed from that language in the tenth century. As Borges says, Averroës "worked on the translation of a translation." If this was the case, then the Córdoban philosopher had an Arabic version in front of him. How then did he stumble on the words *tragoedia* and *comoedia*? We would expect to find their equivalents in Arabic.

There is then a degree of incertitude in Borges's text. We get the impression that Averroës, who knows no Greek, is working on the Greek text of the *Poetics* and that it was his personal responsibility to translate the two doubtful words. It is as though it were with him that the question of their translation had been posed for the first time in Arabic cultural history and that he thus had the responsibility to translate them into Arabic. This is confirmed at the end of the tale, when Averroës, returning from a dinner with "the Qur'ānist Farach," had a revelation: "Something had revealed to him the meaning of the two obscure words. With a firm and neat calligraphy he added these lines to his manuscript: Aristū (Aristotle) labels as 'tragedy' panegyrics and as 'comedy' satires and anathemas. Admirable tragedies and comedies abound in the pages of the Qur'ān and in the sanctuary's *mu'allaqāt*."

But to what manuscript did Averroës add these lines? The only one referred to at the beginning of the tale is *Tahāfut al-tahāfut*, a book that has nothing to do with the *Poetics*. What Borges does not mention is that Averroës most certainly spoke of "two doubtful words," but in another book in which he summarized Aristotle's work.

Let us look once again at what Borges wrote—namely that Averroës had in vain "consulted the versions of the Nestorian Hunayn ibn Ishāq and of Abu Bashar Meta." It would seem that Arabic versions of Aristotle's *Poetics* were involved. If that is the case, then Averroës need not have agonized over finding Arabic equivalents for *tragoedia* and *comoedia*: he would have found them as part of those two translations.

We should, however, point out that Hunayn ibn Ishāq translated many Greek scientific treatises, notably those composed by Hippocrates and Galen, but no source states that he translated Aristotle's *Poetics*. In fact, it was his son, Ishāq ibn Hunayn, who took that task on, but his work unfortunately has never reached us. As for Abu Bashar Meta, he is none other than the Nestorian Abū Bishr Matta (d. 940), who did indeed translate the *Poetics*. It is he, let us repeat, and not Averroës, who was the first person to translate *tragoedia* as "panegyric" and *comoedia* as "satire."

In the final analysis, Borges describes a lost opportunity: Averroës missed a rendezvous with theater. However, he is shown at the beginning of the tale as having attended an extraordinary show: "Through the bars of the balcony he saw some half-naked children playing down below, in the narrow yard. One of them, standing on the shoulders of the other, was obviously playing the role of a muezzin. With his eyes shut tight, he was chanting: 'There is no God but Allah.' The boy who was carrying him on his shoulders, standing stock-still, symbolized the minaret; another boy, prostrate in the dust and kneeling, represented the congregational faithful." Here Borges is pointing out the blindness of the Córdoban philosopher, unable to discern what is clearly visible. Before his very eyes he has a theatrical representation, and yet he does not even realize it.

Later, during dinner at Farach's place, the conversation revolves around Arabic poetry. A foreign touch is introduced by Abul Qāssim, a traveler who claims to have seen the following spectacle in China ("which he barely remembers and which he found most boring"): "One evening Muslim merchants of Sin Kalan took me to a painted wooden house where many people were living.[. . .] The people on the terrace were playing drums and lutes, except for about fifteen or twenty (wearing crimson masks), who were praying, chanting, and conversing. They were in prison, but no one saw their cells; they were on horseback, but no one saw their mounts; they fought, but their swords were made of reeds; they were dying, but they stood up again right away."

This tale is met with incomprehension on the audience's part: "They were not crazy," Abul Qāssim feels compelled to clarify. "A merchant told me they were presenting a story." However, the clarification did not clear up the misunderstanding: "In this case," concludes Farach, "there was no need for twenty people. One narrator can tell anything, no matter how complex it is."

The theme of blindness, often favored by Borges, manifests itself in many ways in the tale. It is not by chance that Ibn Sīda, the blind grammarian, is mentioned, as well as the lexicographer Jalil's [al-Khalil's] *Quitab-ul-ain* [*Kitāb al-ʻayn*]. It is the first Arabic dictionary, with its ambiguous title: *The Book of ʻAyn.* It carries that title because it does not use alphabetical order but rather starts with the letter ع [ʻayn]. However, that particular letter (or word) also means "eye." Later, during dinner, the name "Ibn Sharaf" is mentioned. A poet who was also a critic, he was cross-eyed and indeed was the rival of Ibn Rashīq, who was one-eyed. As for Chahiz (al-Jāhiz), also mentioned during the evening, he owes his name (or rather his nickname) to an ocular peculiarity: he had bulging corneas. Nor is that all. The tale also contains a long disquisition on a line of poetry by the pre-Islamic poet Zuhayr, who compares "destiny to a blind camel." In fact, it is more a matter of death, which is compared to a she-camel that cannot see at night and does not know upon what kind of soil it is treading. Finally, we read that "the muezzins called for the first prayer at dawn when Averroës returned to his library." The chanting does not remind him of the scene in which children were acting out the prayer (and here we should remember that the child who imitates the muezzin has "his eyes shut tight").

According to his biographers, Averroës worked at night. There were only two nights on which he did not work, the night when he was married and the night his father died. During the daytime, he served as a *qadi* (judge): that was the time for the religious law, and its space was the outdoors, the external world. At night, however, he studied philosophy, an almost clandestine discipline that requires solitude and withdrawal, at home, in one's own house, the domain of shadows. He thus participated in two forms of knowledge, each one of which has its own space and time.

However, in Borges's tale, day and night take on particular meanings. At first Averroës is at home, devoting his day to his book against al-Ghazālī. In a second segment: at the end of the day, he goes to Farach's place and spends the night conversing with his friends. Finally, the third part sees him going home; it is dawn, a blending of day and night. It is at that moment that Averroës receives the (deceptive) revelation concerning the meaning of *tragoedia* and *comoedia*, which he confuses with "panegyric" and "satire."

Under the hues of sameness he saw difference. He imported Greek literature into Arabic literature. Averroës left his library and moved toward the others. However, he ended up going back home, returning to his house, the symbol of an attachment to the past, traditional values, the origin, the oriental palm tree. Averroës turned to look back and, in doing so, he lost his Eurydice.

Works Cited

Al-Azdi, Abu-l-Mutahhar. 1902. *Hikāyāt Abī-l-Qāsim al-Baghdādī* (The story of Abu al-Qasim of Baghdad). Translated by Adam Mez. Heidelberg: Carl Winter.

Benabdelali, 'Abdesslam. 2006. *De la traduction.* Casablanca: Toubkal.

Benabdelali, Naima. 1999. *Le Don et l'anti-économique dans la société arabo-musulmane.* Casablanca: Eddif.

Bencheikh, Jamal Eddine, André Miquel, and Claude Bremond. 1991. *Mille et un contes de la nuit.* Paris: Gallimard.

Berque, Jacques. 1958. *Al-Yosi: Problèmes de la culture marocaine au XVIIème siècle.* Paris: Mouton.

———. 1982. "L'Homme qui voulut être roi." In *Ulémas, fondateurs, insurgés du Maghreb: XVIIe siècle,* 45–80. Paris: Sindbad.

Biberstein Kazimirski, Albert de. 1860. *Dictionnaire français-arabe.* Paris: Maisonneuve.

———, trans. 1970. *Le Coran.* Paris: Garnier-Flammarion.

Borges, Jorge Luis. 1993. *Œuvres complètes.* 2 vols. Paris: Gallimard (Bibliothèque de la Pléiade).

Brockelmann, Carl. 1978. "*Kalīla wa-Dimna.*" In *Encyclopaedia of Islam,* new ed., edited by Clifford E. Bosworth, E. van Donzel, Bernard Lewis, and Charles Pellat, 4:503–6. Leiden: E. J. Brill.

Combs-Schilling, M. E. 1989. *Sacred Performances: Islam, Sexuality, and Sacrifice.* New York: Columbia Univ. Press.

Curtius, Ernest Robert. 1973. *European Literature and the Latin Middle Ages.* Translated from the German by Willard R. Trask. Princeton, NJ: Princeton Univ. Press.

Dīwān al-Mu'tamid ibn 'Abbād. 2002. Edited by Malik Ishbīlīyah, Ḥāmid 'Abd al-Majīd, and Aḥmad Aḥmad Badawī. Cairo: Dār al-kutub wa-al wathā'iq al-qawmīyah, Markaz taḥqīq al-turāth.

Ettinghausen, Richard. 1962. *Arab Painting*. [Geneva]: Skira, distributed by World Publishing.

Fradkin, Hillel. 1992. "The Political Thought of Ibn Tufayl." In *The Political Aspects of Islamic Philosophy*, edited by Charles E. Butterworth, 234–61. Cambridge, MA: Harvard Univ. Press.

Fumey, Eugène, trans. 1906–1907. "Chronique de la dynastie Allaouie du Maroc." In *Archives marocaines*, 9–10:n.p. Paris: Ernest Leroux.

Galland, Antoine. 1965. *Les Mille et une nuits*. 3 vols. Paris: Garnier-Flammarion.

Gauthier, Léon. 1909. *Ibn Thofaïl, sa vie, ses œuvres*. Paris: Presses univ. de France.

———. 1936. *Hayy ben Yaqdhân: Roman philosophique d'Ibn Thofaïl*. 2nd ed. Beirut: Imprimerie Catholique.

Al-Ghazālī. 1959. *Erreur et délivrance* (*Al-Munqidh min al-ḍalal*). Translated by Farid Jabre. Beirut: Commission internationale pour la traduction des chefs-d'œuvre.

Ghazoul, Ferial J. 1996. *Nocturnal Poetics*. Cairo: American Univ. in Cairo Press.

Goytisolo, Juan. 1994. *Quarantine*. Translated from the Spanish by Peter Bush. Normal, IL: Dalkey Archive Press.

Grunebaum, Gustave E. von. 1971. "*I'djāz*." In *Encyclopaedia of Islam*, new ed., edited by Bernard Lewis, V. L. Ménage, Charles Pellat, and Joseph Schacht, 3:1018–20. Leiden: E. J. Brill; London: Luzac.

Hamori, Andras. 1974. "The Pre-Islamic *Qasīda*: The Poet as Hero." In *On the Art of Medieval Arabic Literature*, 3–30. Princeton NJ: Princeton Univ. Press.

Al-Harīrī. 1992. *Le Livre des malins: Séances d'un vagabond de génie*. Translated by René Khawam. Paris: Phébus.

Huet, Pierre-Daniel, Jean Chapelain, and Fabienne Gégou, eds. 1971. *Lettre-traité de Pierre-Daniel Huet sur l'origine des romans*. Paris: Nizet.

Ibn Ḥazm, 'Alī ibn Aḥmad. 1931. *The Dove's Neck-Ring, about Love and Lovers*. Translated by A. R. Nykl from the unique manuscript at the University of Leiden. Edited by D. K. Pétrof in 1914. Paris: P. Geuthner.

Ibn al-Muqaffa'. 1964. *Al-adab al-kabir* (The great learning). Edited by Yūsuf Abū Ḥalqah 'Abdu'llāh. Beirut: Manshūrāt maktabat al-Bayān.

Ibn al-Nadim. c. 1970. *The Fihrist of al-Nadīm: A Tenth-Century Survey of Muslim Culture*. Edited and translated by Bayard Dodge. New York: Columbia Univ. Press.

Ibn Qutaybah. 1962. *Le traité des divergences du hadīṯ d'Ibn Qutayba* (*Kitāb ta'wil mukhtalif al-hadith*). Translated by Gérard Lecomte. Damascus: Institut français de Damas.

Ibn Tufayl. 1936. *Hayy Ibn Yaqzān*. Edited by Léon Gauthier. Beirut: Catholic Press.

Al-Ibshīlī. 1981. *Al-mustatraf*. Edited by Ahmad Akram at-Tabba'. Beirut: Dar al-qalam.

Ifrānī, Muḥammad al-Ṣaghīr ibn Muḥammad. 1998. *Nuzhat al-hādī*. Rabat, Morocco: Maktabat at-tālib.

Izutsu, Toshihiko. 1964. *God and Man in the Koran*. Tokyo: Keio Institute of Cultural and Linguistic Studies.

Al-Jāhiz. 1997. *Le Livre des avares*. Translated by Charles Pellat. Paris: Maisonneuve et Larose.

———. 1999. *Avarice & the Avaricious*. Translated from the Arabic with a short introduction and notes by Jim Colville. London: Kegan Paul; New York: Columbia Univ. Press.

———. 2000. *The Book of Misers*. Translated by Robert B. Serjeant. Reading, U.K.: Garnet.

———. 2003a. *Kitāb al-bayān wa-al-tabyīn* (Book of clarity and clarification). Edited by Ibrāhīm Shams al-Dīn. Beirut: Mu'assasat al-A'lami lil-matbu'at.

———. 2003b. *Kitāb al-ḥayawān* (Book of animals). Edited by Ibrāhīm Shams al-Dīn. Beirut: Mu'assasat al-A'lami lil-matbu'at.

Jeanneret, Michel. 1991. *A Feast of Words: Banquets and Table Talk in the Renaissance.* Translated by Jeremy Whiteley and Emma Hughes. Chicago: Univ. of Chicago Press.

Al-Jirārī, 'Abbās. 1981. *'Abqariyyat al-Yousi.* Casablanca: Dār ath-thaqāfa.

Jung, Carl G., and Charles Kerényi. 1980. *Introduction à l'essence de la mythologie.* Translated by Henri E. Del Medico. Paris: Petite bibliothèque Payot.

Kilito, Abdelfattah. 1992. *L'Œil et l'aiguille.* Paris: La Découverte.

———. 2001. *The Author and His Doubles.* Translated by Michael Cooperson. Syracuse, NY: Syracuse Univ. Press.

———. 2008. *Thou Shalt Not Speak My Language.* Translated by Waïl S. Hassan. Syracuse, NY: Syracuse Univ. Press.

Laroui, Abdallah. 1986. "Islam et état." In *Islam et modernité,* 11–46. Paris: La Découverte.

Lavisse, Ernest. 1978. *Louis XIV.* Paris: Tallandier.

Machiavelli, Niccolò. 2003. *The Prince and Other Writings.* Translated and introduced by Wayne A. Rebhorn. New York: Barnes & Noble Classics.

Makki, Tahir Ahmad. 1980. *Dirāsāt 'an Ibn Ḥazm wa-kitābihi "Ṭawq al-ḥamāmah"* ("Preface" of *Tawq al-hamāmah*). Cairo: Dar al-Ma'arif.

Mallet, Dominique. 1997. "Les livres de Hayy." *Arabica* 44, no. 1: 1–34.

———. 1999. "A[b]sal and Joseph, symboles et narration dans le *Hayy b. Yaqzān.*" In *Les Intellectuels en Orient musulman,* edited by Floréal Sanagustin, 67–76. Paris: Institut français d'archéologie orientale.

Mardrus, J. C., trans. 1980. *Le Livre des mille nuits et une nuit.* 16 vols. Paris: Éditions de la Revue blanche.

Al-Mas'ūdī. 1841. *Meadows of Gold and Mines of Gems.* Translated by Aloys Sprenger. London: Oriental Translation Fund of Great Britain and Ireland.

Mauss, Marcel. 1979. *Essay on the Gift.* Part 4 of *Sociology and Psychology: Essays*, translated by Ben Brewster. Boston: Routledge and Kegan Paul.

Miquel, André. 1981. *La Littérature arabe.* Paris: Presses univ. de France.

Müller, Paul Johannes. 1979. *Miniatures arabes: Introduction, choix et textes de présentation.* Paris: Éditions Siloé.

Al-Nīsābūrī, al-Ḥasan ibn Muḥammad. 1987. *'Uqalā' al-majānīn.* Edited by 'Umar al-As'ad. Beirut: Dar an-nafā'is.

Pagis, Dan. 1990. "The Poet as a Prophet in Medieval Hebrew Literature." In *Poetry and Prophecy*, edited by James L. Kugel, 140–50. Ithaca, NY: Cornell Univ. Press.

Pellat, Charles. 1952. *Langue et littérature arabes.* Paris: Armand Colin.

Perec, George. 1973. "Histoire du Lipogramme." In *OuLiPo: La Littérature potentielle (créations, re-créations, récréations)*, 84. Paris: Gallimard.

———. 1987. *Life: A User's Manual (La Vie mode d'emploi).* Translated from the French by David Bellos. Boston: David R. Godine.

Al-Qaddūriī, 'Abd al-Majīd. 1991. *Ibn Abī Mahalī al-faqih al-thā'ir.* Rabat, Morocco: 'Ukād.

Qādirī, Muḥammad ibn al-Ṭayyib. 1977–86. *Nashr al-Mathānī.* Edited by Muhammad Hajji and Ahmad Tawfiq. Rabat, Morocco: Dar al-Maghrib li-al-ta'līf wa-al-tarjama wa-al-nashr.

Al-Qayrawani, Ibn Sharaf. 1955. *Questions de critique littéraire.* Translated into French by Charles Pellat. Algiers: Carbonel.

Rank, Otto. 1959. *The Myth of the Birth of the Hero.* New York: Vintage Books.

Renan, Ernest. 1859. *Essais de morale et de critique.* Paris: Calmann-Lévy.

Sanagustin, Floréal. 1999. *Les Intellectuels en Orient musulman: Statut & fonction.* Cairo: Institut français d'archéologie orientale.

Schlegel, Friedrich von. 1998. *Philosophical Fragments*. Translated by Peter Firchow. Minneapolis: Univ. of Minnesota Press.

Sharīshī, Ahmad ibn Abd al-Mumin. 1952–53. *Sharh maqāmāt al-Harīrī*. 4 vols. Cairo: Al-Muniriyah.

Steiner, George. 1998. *After Babel*. New York: Oxford Univ. Press.

Strauss, Leo. 1975. *On Tyranny*. Ithaca, NY: Cornell Univ. Press.

———. 1988. *Persecution and the Art of Writing*. Chicago: Univ. of Chicago Press.

Tekin, Gönül Alpay. 1995. "Risāla." In *Encyclopaedia of Islam*, new ed., edited by Clifford E. Bosworth, E. van Donzel, Wolfhart P. Heinrichs, and Gerard Lecomte, 8:532–44. Leiden: E. J. Brill.

Todorov, Tzvetan. 1999. "Les Jeux de mots." In *Genres in Discourse*, 294–30. New York: Cambridge Univ. Press.

Vincent-Buffault, Anne. 1985. *Histoire des larmes*. Paris: Rivages.

———. 1991. *The History of Tears: Sensibility and Sentimentality in France*. Translated from the French by Teresa Bridgeman. New York: St. Martin's Press.

Yusī, al-Hasan ibn Mas'ud. 1981. *Rasā'il*. Edited by Fātima Khalil al-Qibli. 2 vols. Casablanca: Dar ath-thaqafa.

———. 1982. *Muhādarāt fi al-adab wa l-lughah*. Edited by Muhammad Hajji and Aḥmad al-Sharqāwī Iqbāl. Beirut: Dar al-gharb al-Islāmī.

Abdelfattah Kilito is an acclaimed Moroccan novelist, essayist, and critic. He was born in Rabat, Morocco, in 1945; obtained a PhD from the new Sorbonne in 1982; and has been teaching literature at the University of Muhammad V in Rabat since 1968. He has written several important works on classical Arabic literature, both in French and in Arabic. His works have been translated into many languages, including French, German, Spanish, Italian, and English. He is the recipient of many awards, including the French Academy Award (Le Prix du rayonnement de la langue française) in 1996.

Eric Sellin is professor emeritus at Tulane University (New Orleans) and lives in Philadelphia. Author of books on Antonin Artaud and early-twentieth-century avant-garde movements, Sellin has also published hundreds of articles and translations as well as a half-dozen collections of poetry (three in French). In 1999, the Council of International Francophone Studies awarded Sellin a certificate of honor "in recognition of his exceptional contributions to the development of francophone studies throughout the world."

Mbarek Sryfi is a lecturer at the University of Pennsylvania and an adjunct assistant professor at Mercer County Community College in New Jersey. His translations have appeared in *CELAAN*, *Metamorphoses*, *Mead Magazine*, *World Literature Today*, and *Banipal*.